# Gooseberry Patch

# *Everyday* Comfort Food

Double-Cheese Scalloped
Potatoes, page 230

# Gooseberry Patch Co. Everyday Comfort Food

## 260

### Easy homestyle recipes for every weeknight

Oxmoor House

## Dear Friend,

There's no better feeling than being able to enjoy home-cooked food, right in the comfort of your own kitchen. But at the end of a busy day, finding the time and energy to make delicious comfort food can be hard. With *Gooseberry Patch Everyday Comfort Food,* you'll find easy, family-pleasing recipes that will be ready in no time. Packed with more than 260 comforting, crave-satisfying recipes, you'll be able to treat your family to a delicious meal any time of day.

They say breakfast is the most important meal of the day, so make sure that everyone starts the morning off right with Hearty Sausage & Egg Bake (page 31). For a quick weeknight dinner, try Cheesy Chicken Fettuccine (page 48). Pair it with the Italian Salad Bowl (page 159) and some fresh bread, and you've got an Italian meal in minutes! Break out your slow cooker and come home to a steaming pot of Potato-Corn Chowder (page 78) on a winter night. We've even included a whole celebrations chapter full of recipes such as the Pork & Raspberry Sauce (page 215) that are sure to impress friends and family at any holiday. And don't forget dessert...Just Peachy Blueberry Crisp (page 177) is the perfect summer treat to satisfy a sweet tooth.

*Everyday Comfort Food* is your go-to guide for those recipes passed down from generation to generation, shared at potlucks or handed over from neighbors. This collection of recipes offers a variety of methods and meals, including slow-cooker recipes, weeknight options, one-dish meals and an array of sides and desserts. So sit down, relax and enjoy some feel-good food from *Everyday Comfort Food.*

### Wishing you delicious dinners,

## Jo Ann & Vickie
co-founders of Gooseberry Patch

# contents

Mary Ann's Sunrise
Egg Bake, page 25

# all about breakfast

Start your day off right with one of these tasty recipes. Everyone will love Spinach & Potato Frittata and Spinach & Bacon Quiche. Try Southern-Style Breakfast Casserole or make a weekend breakfast extra sweet with Farm-Style Cinnamon Rolls. But breakfast foods are so comforting and easy to make, why serve them only in the morning?

# Goldenrod Eggs

*This simple dish will become a favorite comfort food as well as a great holiday breakfast.*

*"Goldenrod Eggs is a family recipe that has been handed down from my Great-Grandmother Rhodes and my Great-Aunt Ruby."*

*—Fawn*

5 to 6 eggs, hard-boiled, peeled and halved
6 T. butter or sausage drippings
6 T. all-purpose flour
2¾ to 3 c. milk
salt and pepper to taste
toast or split biscuits

Place egg yolks in a small bowl; mash and set aside. Chop whites and set aside. Place butter or drippings in a medium saucepan over medium-high heat; when butter is melted or drippings are hot, whisk in flour. Slowly pour in milk to reach desired consistency. Continue to heat through until mixture thickens. Stir in egg whites; season with salt and pepper to taste. Spoon over toast or biscuits. Sprinkle mashed egg yolks over each serving. Serves 4.

Fawn McKenzie
Wenatchee, WA

# Spicy Black Bean Scrambled Eggs

Donna Jones (Mikado, MI)

¼ c. canned black beans, drained
  and rinsed
¼ c. chunky salsa
⅛ t. chili powder
Optional: ⅛ t. red pepper flakes

2 eggs, beaten
6-inch corn tortilla, warmed
¼ c. shredded sharp Cheddar
  cheese
Optional: additional salsa

Spray a small skillet with non-stick vegetable spray. Add beans, salsa and desired seasonings; cook over medium heat one minute, stirring frequently. Add eggs; stir to combine. Continue cooking and stirring until eggs are fully cooked. Spoon egg mixture onto tortilla. Top with cheese and additional salsa, if desired. Serve immediately. Serves one.

Herbed Salmon
Omelets

# Herbed Salmon Omelets

¼ c. sour cream
2 T. fresh dill, chopped
2 T. fresh chives, chopped
2 T. butter, divided

¼ lb. smoked salmon, chopped
   and divided
6 eggs, beaten and divided

Mix together sour cream and herbs in a small bowl; set aside. Melt one tablespoon butter in a small skillet over low heat. Add half the salmon; cook and stir one minute. Add half the eggs to skillet and cook, lifting edges to allow uncooked egg to flow underneath. When almost set, spoon half the sour cream mixture over half the omelet. Fold other half over and slide onto plate. Keep warm while making second omelet with remaining ingredients. Serves 2.

Carrie O'Shea
Marina del Rey, CA

# Creamy Scrambled Eggs + Chives

8 eggs
2 T. fresh chives, chopped
½ t. salt
¼ t. pepper

¼ c. water
2 t. butter
½ c. cream cheese, diced

In a bowl, whisk together eggs with chives, salt, pepper and water; set aside. Melt butter in a skillet over medium-high heat; pour in egg mixture. As eggs begin to set, push them gently toward center with a spatula so that uncooked egg can flow toward sides of skillet. When eggs are partially set, add cream cheese. Continute cooking one more minute, or until eggs are set but still moist, stirring occasionally. Serves 4.

Regina Vining
Warwick, RI

"My husband's brother lives in Alaska, and last summer our family reunion was held there. The men went fishing all day, and the ladies crafted, shopped and tried to find new ways to prepare the bounty of fish being brought home! This recipe was one we enjoyed many times...it's delicious and couldn't be easier to make."

—Carrie

# Simply Scrumptious Frittata

*This is a tasty way to use any remaining ham from Sunday dinner.*

## toss-ins for a twist

Bacon can be substituted for the ham. And you can try a different type of cheese, such as Swiss or mozzarella.

1 T. vegetable oil
½ c. onion, chopped
½ c. green pepper, chopped
1 to 2 cloves garlic, minced
4 Yukon Gold potatoes, cubed and cooked

¾ c. cooked ham, cubed
8 eggs, beaten
salt and pepper to taste
¾ c. shredded Cheddar cheese

Heat oil in a large, heavy oven-proof skillet over medium heat. Add onion and green pepper; cook until tender. Add garlic; cook one more minute. Stir in potatoes and ham; cook until heated through. Reduce heat to medium-low; add eggs, salt and pepper. Cook 5 minutes, or until eggs are firm on the bottom. Top eggs with cheese; bake at 350 degrees for 5 to 10 minutes, until cheese melts. Cut into wedges to serve. Serves 4.

Jill Valentine
Jackson, TN

# Spinach + Potato Frittata

*A tip to remove the moisture from cooked spinach...lay a few paper towels on the counter and place spinach in a single layer on top. Place another layer or two of paper towels over the spinach, roll and squeeze dry.*

6 egg whites
3 eggs
1½ c. potato, peeled, diced
   and cooked
2 slices Canadian bacon, diced
6 c. baby spinach, cooked,
   drained and squeezed dry

½ t. salt
¼ t. pepper
½ c. onion, chopped
2 T. shredded Cheddar cheese

Beat together egg whites and eggs in a large bowl. Stir in potato, Canadian bacon, spinach, salt and pepper. Spray a 9" oven-proof skillet with non-stick vegetable spray; place over medium-high heat. Add onion; sauté 4 minutes, or until tender. Add potato mixture to pan; cook over medium heat 5 minutes, or until almost set. Sprinkle with cheese. Bake at 400 degrees for 6 minutes, or until set. Let stand 3 minutes; slice into quarters. Serves 4.

Lynn Williams
Muncie, IN

## serving suggestion

Fresh fruit is a perfect pairing with early-morning recipes. Set out plump strawberries, juicy oranges, peach slices and fresh berries to enjoy with favorite breakfast dishes. Serve with a bowl of sugar or cream alongside...just to make it extra special.

# Festive Brunch Frittata

Renae Scheiderer (Beallsville, OH)

8 eggs
½ t. salt
⅛ t. pepper
½ c. shredded Cheddar cheese

2 T. butter
2 c. red, green and yellow
   peppers, chopped
¼ c. onion, chopped

Beat together eggs, salt and pepper. Fold in cheese and set aside. Melt butter in a 10" non-stick, oven-proof skillet over medium heat. Add peppers and onion to skillet; sauté until tender. Pour egg mixture over peppers and onion; do not stir. Reduce heat to medium-low. Cover and cook about 9 minutes, until eggs are set and frittata is lightly golden on the underside. Broil with top of frittata about 5 inches from heat for 5 minutes, or until lightly golden. Cut into wedges to serve. Serves 6.

# Easy Bacon Frittata

*Delicious and so simple to put together! Pair with fruit salad for brunch or a crisp green salad for an easy dinner.*

2 c. frozen shredded
  hashbrowns
3 T. vegetable oil
7 eggs, beaten

2 T. milk
12 slices bacon, crisply cooked
  and crumbled
¾ c. shredded Cheddar cheese

Add hashbrowns and oil to a large skillet over medium heat. Cook 10 to 15 minutes, stirring often, until potatoes are golden; drain. Whisk together eggs and milk in a bowl. Pour egg mixture over potatoes; sprinkle with bacon. Cover and reduce heat to low. Cook 10 minutes longer, or until eggs are set. Sprinkle with cheese; cover and cook about 5 minutes, or until cheese is melted. Cut into wedges to serve. Serves 6.

Beth Bundy
Long Prairie, MN

## make-ahead magic

Save time and clean-up…bake the bacon ahead of time! Arrange slices on a jelly-roll pan. Bake at 350 degrees for 15 to 20 minutes, until done to desired crispiness. Drain well on paper towels.

# Sausage Brunch Bake

3 c. herb-flavored croutons
8-oz. pkg. shredded Cheddar
  cheese, divided
½ lb. ground pork breakfast
  sausage, browned and drained
4 eggs, beaten

2½ c. milk, divided
¾ t. dry mustard
10¾-oz. can cream of
  mushroom soup
32-oz. pkg. frozen shredded
  hashbrowns, thawed

Spread croutons in an aluminum foil-lined 13"x9" baking pan. Top croutons with 1½ cups cheese and sausage; set aside. Combine eggs, 2 cups milk and mustard; pour over all. Cover and refrigerate overnight. Combine soup with remaining milk; pour over mixture. Spread hashbrowns over top; sprinkle with remaining cheese. Bake, uncovered, at 325 degrees for one hour. Serves 8 to 10.

Jill Valentine
Jackson, TN

# Herbed Sausage Quiche

*For a savory pie crust, spread 2½ tablespoons softened butter in a pie plate and firmly press 2½ cups buttery cracker crumbs or seasoned dry bread crumbs into the butter. Freeze until firm; pour in filling and bake as directed.*

9-inch frozen pie crust, thawed
1 c. ground pork breakfast
  sausage, browned and
  drained
3 eggs, beaten
1 c. whipping cream

1 c. shredded Cheddar cheese
1 sprig fresh rosemary,
  chopped
1½ t. Italian seasoning
¼ t. salt
¼ t. pepper

Bake pie crust according to package directions. Mix together remaining ingredients in a bowl; spread into crust. Bake, uncovered, at 450 degrees for 15 minutes. Reduce oven temperature to 350 degrees, cover with aluminum foil and bake 9 more minutes. Cut into wedges to serve. Serves 8.

Cherylann Smith
Efland, NC

## serving suggestion

For a brunch buffet, serve an assortment of artisan cheeses. Line a white-washed basket with red and white homespun, tie a red bow on the handle and fill it with a variety of cheeses and crackers. Perfect for guests to nibble on…they may even discover a new favorite or two!

## perfect crust

Baking the pie crust before you add all of the ingredients keeps the bottom of the quiche from becoming soggy. You can also brush egg whites over the bottom of the crust before adding the liquid ingredients to ward off sogginess.

# Spinach + Bacon Quiche

*This classic combination is always popular with a side of grapes or sliced melon.*

4 slices bacon, crisply cooked
  and crumbled, drippings
  reserved
½ c. onion, thinly sliced
2 c. baby spinach
9-inch refrigerated pie crust

½ c. fontina cheese, shredded
5 eggs, beaten
½ c. milk
¼ c. whipping cream
salt and pepper to taste
⅛ t. nutmeg

Heat reserved drippings in a large skillet over medium heat. Add onion; cook about 3 minutes, or until tender. Add spinach, one cup at a time; cook about one minute, just until wilted. Cool. Sprinkle bottom of pie crust with cheese. Evenly distribute bacon and spinach mixture over cheese. Whisk together eggs, milk, whipping cream, salt, pepper and nutmeg in a bowl. Pour over bacon and spinach mixture. Bake at 375 degrees for 25 to 35 minutes; cool 5 to 10 minutes before cutting into wedges to serve. Serves 6 to 8.

# Crustless Bacon-Swiss Quiche

*With one less step, this quiche recipe is a real time-saver.*

9 eggs, beaten
3 c. milk
1 t. dry mustard
salt and pepper to taste
9 slices white bread, crusts
   trimmed

1½ c. Swiss cheese, diced
1 lb. bacon, crisply cooked and
   crumbled

Combine eggs, milk, mustard, salt and pepper in a large bowl; blend well. Tear bread into small pieces; add to egg mixture along with cheese and bacon. Spoon into a greased 13"x9" baking pan or 2 greased 9" glass pie plates. Cover and refrigerate 2 hours to overnight. Uncover and bake at 350 degrees for 45 to 50 minutes, until eggs have set. Cut into squares or wedges. Serves 12.

Sharon Monroe
Concord, NH

## serving suggestion

No need to slice and serve… bake a quiche in muffin or custard cups for oh-so simple individual servings. When baking minis, reduce the baking time by about 10 minutes, and slide a toothpick into each to check for doneness.

# Cheddar + Bacon Breakfast Sandwiches

*Substitute Monterey Jack or Swiss cheese for a change in flavor.*

3 eggs
¼ c. milk
2 T. butter
8 thick slices bread

12 slices Cheddar cheese
1½ t. chopped walnuts
4 slices bacon, crisply cooked and crumbled

Beat together eggs and milk in a large bowl; set aside. Melt butter in a griddle or large skillet over low heat. Dip only one side of 4 bread slices in egg mixture. Place 4 bread slices, coated side down, on griddle or in skillet. Top each bread slice with 3 cheese slices. Sprinkle cheese evenly with walnuts and bacon. Dip only one side of the remaining 4 bread slices in egg mixture and place over walnuts and bacon, coated side up. Cook 5 minutes per side, or until bread is golden and cheese is melted. Serves 4.

Vickie
Gooseberry Patch

# California Omelet

*"I enjoyed trying a similar omelet in El Cajon, California, while visiting my cousin there. I just had to try my hand at making my own version of it...this is the yummy result!"*

*—Christina*

1 T. oil
3 to 4 eggs
¼ c. milk
salt and pepper to taste
1 avocado, pitted, peeled and diced

2 to 3 green onions, diced
1 tomato, diced
½ c. shredded Monterey Jack cheese

Heat oil in a skillet over medium-low heat. Beat together eggs, milk, salt and pepper in a bowl; pour into skillet. Cook 6 to 8 minutes, until eggs are lightly golden on bottom and partially set on top. Sprinkle with remaining ingredients; carefully fold omelet in half to cover toppings. Reduce heat to low and cook, uncovered, about 10 minutes. Serves 2.

Christina Mendoza
Alamogordo, NM

California
Omelet

# Sunrise Ham Quiche

## toss-ins for a twist

Along with the mushrooms, you can add some fresh vegetables from your garden or that you have on hand in your refrigerator. Chopped tomatoes and sliced onions, for example, make tasty additions.

1 c. cooked ham, diced
1 T. butter
1 c. sliced mushrooms
4 eggs
1 c. sour cream
1 c. cottage cheese
½ c. fresh Parmesan cheese, grated
¼ c. all-purpose flour
½ t. dill weed
½ t. dry mustard
⅛ t. nutmeg
⅛ t. pepper
1 c. shredded Swiss cheese
½ c. fresh parsley, chopped
Garnish: fresh dill

Cook ham in a skillet over medium-high heat 6 to 8 minutes, until slightly browned; remove from skillet to a small bowl and set aside. Melt butter in the same skillet over medium-high heat; sauté mushrooms in butter 5 minutes, or until tender. Stir mushrooms into ham and place in a greased 9" pie plate. Combine eggs, sour cream, cottage cheese, Parmesan cheese, flour, dill, mustard, nutmeg and pepper in a blender; cover and blend until smooth. Stir in Swiss cheese and parsley; pour over ham and mushrooms. Bake at 350 degrees for 40 to 45 minutes; let stand 10 minutes before slicing. Garnish with dill. Serves 6 to 8.

Kristi Stahl
Hutchinson, MN

# Country Breakfast Skillet

16-oz. pkg. frozen hashbrowns, thawed
salt and pepper to taste
garlic powder to taste
6 to 8 eggs
⅓ c. milk
1 to 2 tomatoes, chopped

4 to 6 green onions, thinly sliced
¼ lb. thinly sliced deli ham, chopped
1½ c. shredded Cheddar cheese

Cook hashbrowns according to package directions for skillet. Season with salt, pepper and garlic powder; set aside. Beat eggs with milk; add tomatoes, onions and ham. Stir egg mixture into hashbrowns; place over medium heat and stir quickly to scramble. As eggs begin to firm, add cheese and continue to stir until eggs are cooked and set. Makes 4 servings.

Natalie Roberge
Stillwater, MN

## "egg-cellent" presentation

Search for vintage egg cups at tag sales and antique shops…so pretty on the breakfast table or lined up on your kitchen windowsill! These dainty cups are made of everything from hobnail milk glass and porcelain to sterling silver.

# Rise + Shine Torte
Sue Cherry (Starkville, MS)

*An easy gourmet meal that will impress your guests…also try it with mushrooms and spinach.*

2 eggs, beaten
⅓ c. milk
2 T. all-purpose flour
½ t. salt
1 c. sharp Cheddar cheese,
  shredded
1 c. Monterey Jack cheese,
  shredded
4-oz. can diced green chiles

Combine eggs, milk, flour and salt in a large bowl; mix well. Add remaining ingredients, mixing well. Pour into a well-greased 13"x9" baking pan; bake, uncovered, at 350 degrees for 35 minutes. Cut into small squares to serve. Serves 6 to 8.

# Mary Ann's Sunrise Egg Bake

*This is my absolute go-to egg casserole…it is so good! I always make a couple of all-vegetable bakes, too. Try adding onions, colorful red and green peppers and whatever else you like.*

1 doz. eggs
1 c. evaporated milk
2 t. dry mustard
salt and pepper to taste
8-oz. pkg. shredded Cheddar
   cheese

1 c. cooked ham, chopped
8-oz. can sliced mushrooms,
   drained
¼ c. butter, diced

### make-ahead magic

Make and refrigerate this dish the night before. Simply place it in the oven when you wake up for a warm and delicious breakfast.

Beat together eggs, milk, mustard, salt and pepper in a large bowl. Stir in cheese, ham and mushrooms. Pour into a lightly greased 13"x9" baking pan; dot with butter. Bake, uncovered, at 300 degrees for 45 minutes. Cool slightly before cutting into squares. Serves 12.

Kathy Grashoff
Fort Wayne, IN

# Upside-Down Eggs + Potatoes

"My husband's favorite Sunday breakfast! It always makes an impressive presentation yet is deceptively simple to prepare."

—Jessica

2 to 3 T. olive oil
1 to 2 potatoes, shredded
1½ t. garlic powder
1½ t. onion powder
½ t. paprika

1½ c. shredded Mexican blend cheese
6 eggs
salt and pepper to taste
Garnish: sour cream, salsa

Heat oil in a deep 10" oven-proof skillet over medium heat. Pat potatoes dry and place in a bowl; add seasonings and toss to mix. Add potatoes to skillet. When about half cooked, use the back of a wooden spoon to smooth out potatoes over the bottom and up the sides of the skillet to form a crust with no holes. Add cheese in an even layer. Beat eggs very well; add salt and pepper to taste. Gently pour eggs over cheese. Bake, uncovered, at 375 degrees for 20 to 25 minutes, until a knife tip inserted in center comes out clean. Carefully unmold onto a serving plate. Let stand 10 minutes before cutting into wedges. Serve with sour cream and salsa. Serves 6.

Jessica Dekoekkoek
Richmond, VA

## cast-iron secrets

A cast-iron skillet is perfect for cooking up hashbrowns with the crispiest golden crust. If the skillet hasn't been used in a while, season it first...rub it all over with oil and place in a 300-degree oven for an hour. Cool completely before removing from the oven.

# Aimee's Sausage Bake

*It's the apple that makes this breakfast casserole taste so good.*

## serving suggestion

How about setting up a cereal station for breakfast? Pair pitchers of icy-cold milk with a variety of tasty cereals and fruits. You can even have packets of instant oatmeal on hand.

1 doz. eggs, divided
1½ c. milk, divided
1½ c. saltine crackers, crushed
1 c. apple, peeled, cored and chopped
¼ c. onion, chopped
½ t. pepper, divided
2 lbs. ground pork breakfast sausage

3 T. butter
3 T. all-purpose flour
1 c. cottage cheese
½ t. salt
Garnish: chopped fresh parsley, thinly sliced apples

Whisk together 2 eggs and ½ cup milk in a large bowl. Stir in cracker crumbs, apple, onion and ¼ teaspoon pepper. Stir in sausage and mix well. Firmly pat mixture into an ungreased 6½-cup ring mold, and carefully unmold sausage ring onto a wire rack on a greased baking sheet. Bake at 350 degrees for 50 minutes. Transfer to a platter to keep warm. Melt butter in a 3-quart saucepan over medium heat. Whisk in flour until smooth. Add remaining one cup milk all at once. Cook and stir over medium heat until bubbly. Continue to cook and stir 2 more minutes. Beat together remaining eggs and pepper; add cottage cheese and salt in a large bowl. Pour into hot milk mixture. Scramble eggs, stirring frequently, until eggs are cooked through but still moist. Spoon eggs into center of sausage ring and garnish with parsley and apple slices. Serves 12.

Aimee Warner
Marion, OH

# Amish Breakfast Casserole

1 lb. bacon, diced
1 sweet onion, chopped
1 green pepper, diced
10 eggs, beaten
4 c. frozen shredded
  hashbrowns, thawed

2 c. shredded Cheddar cheese
1½ c. cream-style cottage
  cheese
1½ c. shredded Monterey Jack
  cheese, divided

*"I liked to make this hearty dish when my boys came home from college for the holidays."*

*—Barb*

Cook bacon, onion and green pepper in a large skillet over medium heat until bacon is crisp; drain and set aside. Combine remaining ingredients in a large bowl, reserving ¼ cup of the Monterey Jack cheese. Stir bacon mixture into egg mixture. Transfer to a greased 13"x9" baking pan; sprinkle with reserved cheese. Bake, uncovered, at 350 degrees for 35 to 40 minutes, until set and bubbly. Let stand 10 minutes before cutting. Serves 8 to 10.

Barb Bargdill
Gooseberry Patch

# Tex-Mex Sausage Casserole

*A slow-cooker casserole that's ideal for a breakfast with family & friends. For a real kick, add chopped jalapeños to taste!*

1-lb. pkg. ground breakfast
  sausage, browned and
  drained
4-oz. can diced green chiles
1 onion, diced
1 green pepper, diced

2½ c. shredded Monterey Jack
  or Pepper Jack cheese
18 eggs, beaten
Garnish: sour cream, salsa,
  chopped fresh cilantro,
  chopped green onions

Layer half each of sausage, chiles, onion, pepper and cheese in a greased 6-quart slow cooker. Repeat layering. Pour beaten eggs over top. Cover and cook on low setting for 7 to 8 hours. Serve with sour cream and salsa, and garnish with cilantro and green onions. Serves 10.

Vickie
Gooseberry Patch

Hearty Sausage & Egg Bake

# Hearty Sausage + Egg Bake

6-oz. pkg. croutons
2 lbs. ground pork breakfast
    sausage, browned and
    drained
6 eggs
2½ c. milk
1 t. dry mustard
10¾-oz. can cream of
    mushroom soup
8-oz. pkg. shredded Cheddar
    cheese

The night before, sprinkle croutons into a greased 13"x9" baking pan; top with sausage. Beat eggs, milk and mustard in a bowl; pour over sausage. Cover and refrigerate overnight. In the morning, spread soup over casserole; sprinkle with cheese. Bake, uncovered, at 300 degrees for one hour, or until center is done. Serves 16.

Laura Phares
Greenfield, IN

*"This easy-to-fix dish is always a big hit when I serve it at our church's sunrise breakfast...everyone just loves it!"*

*—Laura*

# Rise + Shine Breakfast Pizza

2-lb. pkg. frozen shredded
    hashbrowns
1½ c. shredded Cheddar
    cheese, divided
7 eggs
½ c. milk
salt and pepper to taste
10 to 12 sausage patties,
    cooked

Prepare hashbrowns according to package directions; spread on an ungreased baking sheet or pizza pan. Top with ½ cup cheese; set aside. Whisk together eggs and milk in a microwave-safe bowl; microwave on high 3 minutes, then scramble eggs well with a whisk. Return to microwave and cook 3 more minutes; whisk well to scramble. Layer eggs on top of cheese; add salt and pepper to taste. Top with remaining cheese. Arrange sausage patties on top. Bake at 400 degrees for 10 minutes, or until cheese is melted. Cut into wedges to serve. Serves 8 to 10.

Micki Stephens
Marion, OH

*"Tasty layers of all your breakfast favorites!"*

*—Micki*

Southern-Style
Breakfast Casserole

# Southern-Style Breakfast Casserole

2 lbs. ground pork breakfast
   sausage, browned and
   drained
4 eggs, beaten
1 onion, diced
6 c. crispy rice cereal
2 c. cooked rice
10¾-oz. can cream of
   chicken soup
10¾-oz. can cream of
   celery soup
8-oz. pkg. shredded Cheddar
   cheese
½ c. milk

"If I didn't bring this to breakfast on Palm Sunday, I don't think they'd let me in the door!"

—Joyce

Combine all ingredients in a large bowl. Pour into a lightly greased 13"x9" baking pan. Bake, uncovered, at 400 degrees for 30 minutes. Serves 8 to 10.

Joyce Boswell
Lewisport, KY

# Petite Breakfast Tarts

1 c. all-purpose flour
½ c. butter
3-oz. pkg. cream cheese,
   softened
1 c. pecans, finely chopped
¾ c. brown sugar, packed
1 egg
1 t. vanilla extract
1 T. butter, softened

Place flour in a medium mixing bowl; cut in butter and cream cheese with pastry blender or 2 knives. Chill dough for one hour. Shape dough into one-inch balls and press in lightly oiled small tart pans or mini muffin cups. Sprinkle about one tablespoon chopped pecans into each dough-lined tart pan. Stir together brown sugar, egg, vanilla and one tablespoon butter; spoon mixture over pecans in each pan. Fill each pan slightly less than half full. Bake at 350 degrees for 20 minutes, or until puffy with a golden crust on edges. Makes 1½ to 2 dozen.

Jill Valentine
Jackson, TN

# Smoked Gouda Grits

*These smoky & creamy grits are the perfect addition to scrambled eggs and breakfast sausage...yum!*

6 c. chicken broth
2 c. milk
1 t. salt
½ t. white pepper
2 c. quick-cooking grits, uncooked

1⅔ c. smoked Gouda cheese, shredded
3 T. butter, softened

Bring broth, milk, salt and pepper to a boil in a large saucepan over medium heat. Gradually whisk in grits. Reduce heat; cover and simmer, stirring occasionally, about 5 minutes, until thickened. Add cheese and butter; stir until melted. Serves 6 to 8.

Becky Woods
Ballwin, MO

# Hearty Creamed Eggs + Toast

*A perfect start to any day...so warm & rich!*

2 10¾-oz. cans cream of mushroom soup
milk

6 eggs, hard-boiled, peeled and sliced
8 to 10 slices bread, toasted

Place soup in a large saucepan over medium-high heat; fill empty soup can with milk and add to soup. Add eggs. Continue cooking, stirring frequently, until mixture is warmed but not boiling. Serve over toast. Serves 8 to 10.

Ruby McFarland
Monticello, KY

# Grits Au Gratin
Debi Gilpin (Bluefield, WV)

*Quick and versatile, this side is great for breakfast, lunch or dinner.*

3 c. water
¾ c. quick-cooking grits, uncooked
1 t. salt
¼ lb. sharp Cheddar cheese,
  thinly sliced

½ c. milk
½ c. dry bread crumbs
1 T. butter, melted
¼ t. paprika

Bring 3 cups water to a boil in a saucepan over medium heat; stir in grits and salt. Cook 2½ to 5 minutes; remove from heat. Alternate layers of grits and cheese in a greased 1½-quart casserole dish; pour milk over the top. Toss bread crumbs and butter in a bowl; sprinkle over casserole. Sprinkle with paprika; bake, uncovered, at 325 degrees for 20 to 25 minutes. Serves 4.

Toasted Pecan Pancakes

# Toasted Pecan Pancakes

2 eggs
2 T. sugar
¼ c. butter, melted and
    slightly cooled
¼ c. maple syrup
1½ c. all-purpose flour
2 t. baking powder
½ t. salt
1½ c. milk
⅔ c. chopped pecans, toasted
oil
additional butter; warmed
    maple syrup

Beat together eggs, sugar, butter and syrup in a large bowl. Mix together flour, baking powder and salt in a separate bowl. Add flour mixture and milk alternately to egg mixture, beginning and ending with flour mixture. Stir in pecans. Set a griddle or a large, heavy skillet over medium heat and brush lightly with oil. Griddle is ready when a few drops of water sizzle when sprinkled on the surface. Pour batter by scant ¼ cupfuls onto griddle. Cook until bubbles appear on top of pancakes and bottoms are golden, about 2 minutes. Flip and cook on the other side, about one more minute, until golden. Add a little more oil to griddle for each batch. Serve pancakes with additional butter and warm maple syrup. Makes about 1½ dozen.

Gail Prather
Hastings, NE

*"These very special little pancakes make an ordinary weekend breakfast extraordinary. My kids really enjoy them served with pure maple syrup and sliced ripe bananas on the side!"*

*—Gail*

# Homestyle Potato Pancakes

4 c. mashed potatoes
2 eggs, beaten
2 onions, finely chopped
1 t. salt
½ t. pepper
¼ c. olive oil

Combine potatoes, eggs and onion in a medium mixing bowl; stir well to blend. Add salt and pepper. Heat oil in a large skillet over medium heat. Drop ¼ cupfuls potato mixture into oil and flatten each to ¾-inch thick. Cook each pancake until golden on both sides. Serves about 6.

Vickie
Gooseberry Patch

## Overnight Buttermilk-Raisin Pancakes

*"These pancakes are a breakfast time-saver, so we can enjoy every minute of Christmas morning."*

*—Bev*

2 c. quick-cooking oats, uncooked
2 c. buttermilk
½ c. all-purpose flour
2 T. sugar
1 t. baking powder
1 t. baking soda
½ t. cinnamon

½ t. salt
2 eggs, beaten
¼ c. butter, melted
½ c. raisins
Optional: chopped walnuts, additional raisins
Garnish: syrup

Mix together oats and buttermilk in a medium bowl; cover and refrigerate overnight. Sift together flour, sugar, baking powder, baking soda, cinnamon and salt in a large bowl. Make a well in the center; add oat mixture, eggs, butter and raisins. Stir just until moistened. Allow batter to stand 20 minutes before cooking. If batter is too thick, add buttermilk, one tablespoon at a time, until batter reaches desired consistency. Place a lightly greased large skillet over medium heat. Pour batter by ¼ cupfuls into skillet. Cook pancakes until bubbles appear on top; flip and cook until golden on both sides. Top with walnuts and additional raisins, if desired, and serve with syrup. Serves 9.

Bev Ray
Brandon, FL

# Grandma McKindley's Waffles

*You can't go wrong with an old-fashioned waffle breakfast…the topping choices are endless.*

2 c. all-purpose flour
1 T. baking powder
¼ t. salt
2 eggs, separated

1½ c. milk
3 T. butter, melted
additional butter, syrup

Sift together flour, baking powder and salt in a large bowl; set aside. Beat egg whites with an electric mixer at high speed until stiff; set aside. Stir together egg yolks, milk and melted butter in a separate bowl; add to dry ingredients, stirring just until moistened. Fold in egg whites. Ladle batter by ½ cupfuls onto a lightly greased preheated waffle iron; bake according to manufacturer's directions. Serve wth additional butter and syrup. Serves 4.

Nicole Millard
Mendon, MI

# Apple Crunch Coffee Cake

*This coffee cake stays so moist that you can even make it the night before.*

⅓ c. butter, softened
⅓ c. shortening
2 c. sugar
2 eggs
3 c. all-purpose flour
2 t. baking powder

1 t. cinnamon
½ t. baking soda
¼ t. salt
1¾ c. buttermilk
2 to 3 apples, peeled, cored and sliced

Beat together butter, shortening and sugar in a large bowl until light and fluffy. Add eggs, one at a time, beating well after each addition; set aside. Stir together flour, baking powder, cinnamon, baking soda and salt in a separate bowl; add to butter mixture alternately with buttermilk. Spread half the batter into a greased 13"x9" baking pan; top with apples. Spread remaining batter over apples; sprinkle with Topping. Bake, uncovered, at 350 degrees for 45 to 55 minutes, until a toothpick inserted in center comes out clean. Serves 12.

## Topping:

1 c. all-purpose flour
1 c. brown sugar, packed

1 T. cinnamon
6 T. butter

Stir together flour, brown sugar and cinnamon in a bowl. Cut in butter with a pastry blender or fork until crumbly.

Jill Carr
Sutter Creek, CA

# Farm-Style Cinnamon Rolls

*There's nothing like waking up to the aroma of baking cinnamon rolls.*

16-oz. pkg. frozen bread
  dough, thawed
¼ c. butter, melted and
  divided

¼ c. sugar
¼ c. brown sugar, packed
1 t. cinnamon

## make-ahead magic

Make and freeze this dish ahead for up to one month. Simply freeze the entire roll, thaw and slice before baking.

Place dough in a well-oiled bowl; cover and let rise to almost double its size. Roll out dough on a floured surface to a 14-inch by 10-inch rectangle. Brush with 2 tablespoons butter; sprinkle with sugars and cinnamon. Starting on one long side, roll up jelly-roll style. Pinch seam together. Cut rolled dough into 12 slices. Coat the inside of a 9"x9" baking pan with remaining butter; place dough slices in pan. Cover and let rise in a warm place 45 minutes to one hour. Uncover and bake at 375 degrees for 20 to 25 minutes, until lightly golden. Makes one dozen.

Cindy Adams
Winona Lake, IN

Chicken & Sausage
Skilletini, page 55

# easy weeknight meals

When it's dinnertime, busy families need hearty, homestyle meals that come together in a hurry. Try one-dish winners such as White Chicken Pizza, Cheesy Chicken Fettuccine, Mama's Quick Meatball Subs and Farmhands' Stuffed Sandwich. There's something here to please everyone in the family.

# Chicken Kiev

1½ c. dry bread crumbs
½ c. grated Parmesan cheese
1 t. dried basil
1 t. dried oregano
½ t. garlic salt
½ t. salt
⅔ c. butter, melted and divided
1½ lbs. chicken tenders
¼ c. white wine or chicken broth
¼ c. green onions, chopped
¼ c. dried parsley

Combine bread crumbs, cheese and seasonings in a large bowl. Reserve ¼ cup butter. Dip chicken in remaining melted butter. Roll chicken in crumb mixture. Arrange chicken in a lightly greased 13"x9" baking pan. Bake, covered, at 375 degrees for 30 to 40 minutes, until juices run clear when chicken is pierced. Heat wine or broth, green onions, parsley and reserved butter in a small saucepan over medium heat until heated through. Spoon over chicken and bake, covered, 5 to 7 minutes. Serves 6 to 8.

Grecia Williams
Scottsville, KY

*"My daughters always request this dish when they come home from college."*
*—Grecia*

# Chicken-Artichoke Bake

2 to 3 lbs. boneless, skinless chicken breasts
14½-oz. can chicken broth
14-oz. can artichoke hearts, drained and quartered
¼ c. sliced mushrooms
2 T. butter
¼ t. salt
¼ t. pepper
¾ c. half-and-half
½ c. grated Parmesan cheese
½ t. dried rosemary
¼ c. all-purpose flour

In a large skillet over medium-high heat, simmer chicken in broth until juices run clear when chicken is pierced; discard broth. Place chicken in a greased 13"x9" baking pan. Top with artichokes and mushrooms; set aside. Combine butter, salt, pepper, half-and-half, cheese and rosemary in a saucepan; bring to a boil. Blend in flour; pour over chicken. Bake, uncovered, at 350 degrees for 30 minutes. Serves 6 to 8.

Kristine Kundrick
Fenton, MI

# Mary's Heavenly Chicken

1 c. sour cream
1 T. lemon juice
2 cloves garlic, finely chopped
2 t. celery salt
1 t. paprika
½ t. pepper
2 t. Worcestershire sauce

6 boneless, skinless chicken breasts
1½ c. Italian-flavored dry bread crumbs
¼ c. butter, melted
cooked rice or noodles

Combine sour cream, juice, garlic, celery salt, paprika, pepper and Worcestershire sauce in a large bowl. Add chicken and coat well. Cover and refrigerate overnight. Remove chicken from mixture and roll in bread crumbs. Arrange in a single layer in a lightly greased 15"x10" jelly-roll pan. Spoon melted butter over chicken. Bake, uncovered, at 350 degrees for 25 minutes, or until juices run clear when chicken is pierced. Serve over rice or noodles. Serves 6.

Julie Otto
Fountainville, PA

"My stepmom introduced me to this chicken dish when I was about 10 years old. It's a recipe her neighbor gave to her, hence the name. It has since become a favorite of my husband and many of our family members."

—Julie

# Deb's Chicken Florentine

"My husband loves Italian food! When a local restaurant closed, he was sad that he couldn't get his favorite dish anymore, so I re-created it for him. You can substitute frozen spinach, canned mushrooms or rotisserie chicken. Serve with bread sticks to sop up all the delicious juices."

—Deb

16-oz. pkg. linguine pasta, uncooked
2 T. olive oil
3 cloves garlic, minced
4 boneless, skinless chicken breasts, thinly sliced
1¼ c. fat-free zesty Italian salad dressing, divided

8 sun-dried tomatoes, chopped
8-oz. pkg. sliced mushrooms
5-oz. pkg. baby spinach
cracked pepper to taste
Optional: grated Parmesan cheese, chopped fresh flat-leaf parsley

Cook pasta according to package directions; drain. While pasta is cooking, warm oil in a skillet over medium heat. Add garlic and cook 2 minutes. Add chicken; cook until juices run clear when chicken is pierced. Drizzle chicken with one cup salad dressing. Stir in tomatoes and mushrooms; cover skillet and simmer until mushrooms are softened. Add spinach; cover skillet and cook another 2 to 3 minutes, just until spinach is wilted. Stir and sprinkle with pepper. Toss cooked linguine with remaining ¼ cup salad dressing. Serve chicken and vegetables over linguine. Sprinkle with cheese and parsley, if desired. Serves 6.

Deb Eaton
Mesa, AZ

# White Chicken Pizza
Michelle Schuberg (Big Rapids, MI)

*A quick & easy dinner even your most finicky eater will love!*

13.8-oz. can refrigerated pizza
   crust dough
1 T. olive oil
2 boneless, skinless chicken
   breasts, cubed

2 T. garlic, minced
16-oz. jar Alfredo pasta sauce
½ c. onion, chopped
8-oz. pkg. shredded mozzarella,
   Parmesan & Romano cheese blend

Spread dough onto a lightly greased pizza baking pan; bake at 425 degrees for 7 minutes. Heat oil in a skillet over medium heat; sauté chicken and garlic in oil until juices run clear when chicken is pierced. Pour Alfredo sauce over baked crust; sprinkle with chicken and onion. Bake 10 more minutes; top with cheese blend and return to oven until cheeses melt. Serves 8.

# Cheesy Chicken Fettuccine

10¾-oz. can cream of mushroom soup
8-oz. pkg. cream cheese, cubed
4-oz. can sliced mushrooms, drained
1 c. whipping cream
½ c. butter, melted
¼ t. garlic powder

¾ c. grated Parmesan cheese
½ c. shredded mozzarella cheese
½ c. shredded Swiss cheese
2½ c. cooked chicken, cubed
8-oz. pkg. fettuccine pasta, cooked

Combine soup, cream cheese, mushrooms, whipping cream, butter and garlic powder in a large saucepan over medium heat. Stir in cheeses until melted. Add chicken; heat through. Stir in fettuccine. Spread in a lightly greased 2-quart casserole dish; sprinkle with Topping. Cover and bake at 350 degrees for 25 to 30 minutes, until golden. Serves 8.

## Topping:

⅓ c. seasoned bread crumbs
2 T. butter, melted

1 to 2 T. grated Parmesan cheese

Mix together all ingredients in a small bowl.

Margaret Scoresby
Mosinee, WI

# Creamy Chicken Spaghetti

*"This is one of my husband's favorite meals, and I enjoy making it because it's so quick & easy!"*

—Aimee

2 lbs. chicken breasts, cooked and shredded
16-oz. pkg. spaghetti, cooked
2 14½-oz. cans stewed tomatoes, chopped
2 10¾-oz. cans cream of chicken soup

10¾-oz. can cream of mushroom soup
8-oz. pkg. pasteurized process cheese spread, cubed
4-oz. can mushrooms, drained

Combine all ingredients in a Dutch oven; cook over medium heat until warmed through and cheese is melted. Serves 8.

Aimee Bowlin
Keithville, LA

# Church Bazaar Chicken à la King

*Not only is this absolutely delicious, it's oh-so perfect when you're looking for a recipe that's just right for a large get-together!*

3 c. butter
3½ c. all-purpose flour
salt to taste
6 c. milk, warmed
6 lbs. chicken, cooked and diced

2 8-oz. pkgs. mushrooms, chopped
2 4-oz. jars diced pimentos, drained
cooked rice or noodles
Garnish: chopped fresh parsley

Melt butter in a large saucepan over medium heat; remove from heat. Stir in flour, a little at a time, whisking until smooth. Sprinkle with salt; gradually add warmed milk, whisking constantly. Bring to a boil, stirring until smooth and thick, about 15 to 20 minutes. Stir in chicken, mushrooms and pimentos; simmer until heated through. Serve with rice or noodles. Serves 20.

Wendy Jacobs
Idaho Falls, ID

## for a crowd

When you're planning dinner for a large group, here are some basic quantities to keep in mind. Each dish will feed about 12 people: one gallon of soup, 4 pounds of boneless chicken, 7½ pounds of bone-in roast and 2 pounds of vegetables.

# Country Chicken + Vegetables

*Perfect for a Sunday dinner.*

2 eggplants, peeled and cubed
1 to 2 T. salt
3 c. green beans, cut up
1 c. okra, sliced ½-inch thick
2 onions, sliced
4 green peppers, diced

3½ lbs. chicken
2 to 3 T. oil
2 tomatoes, sliced
2½ c. chicken broth, heated
salt and pepper to taste

Sprinkle eggplant with salt in a bowl; let stand 30 minutes. Layer green beans, okra, onions and green peppers in a greased roasting pan. Rinse eggplant and drain; place over vegetables in roasting pan. Lightly brown chicken in oil in a skillet over medium heat; drain. Arrange chicken over vegetables; top with tomato slices, broth, salt and pepper. Cover and bake at 350 degrees for 1½ to 2 hours, until juices run clear when chicken is pierced and vegetables are tender. Serves 6 to 8.

Tonya Adams
Magnolia, KY

# Bacon-Wrapped Chicken

2 T. chive and onion flavored
  cream cheese, softened and
  divided
2 boneless, skinless chicken
  breasts, flattened to ½-inch
  thickness

2 T. chilled butter, divided
salt and pepper to taste
2 slices bacon

Spread one tablespoon cream cheese over each chicken breast; top with one tablespoon butter and desired amount of seasonings. Roll up and wrap with one slice bacon; secure with a toothpick. Place seam-side down on a rimmed baking sheet; bake at 400 degrees for 35 to 40 minutes, until juices run clear when chicken is pierced with a fork. Serves 2.

Linda Strausburg
Arroyo Grande, CA

# Chicken + Rotini Stir-Fry

*This very tasty, light recipe is so easy to make. You're gonna love it!*

2½ c. rotini pasta, uncooked
2 T. olive oil
2 boneless, skinless chicken
   breasts, cut into strips
1 c. broccoli flowerets
1 c. carrots, peeled and cut into
   curls with a vegetable peeler

½ c. red onion, sliced
¼ c. water
½ t. chicken bouillon granules
½ t. fresh tarragon, snipped
2 T. grated Parmesan cheese

## toss-ins for a twist

Penne pasta, macaroni and bow-tie pasta all make nice substitutions for the rotini pasta in this dish. Use what you have on hand in the pantry. You can also substitute asparagus or green beans for the broccoli if you have them in the refrigerator.

Cook pasta according to package directions; drain. Meanwhile, heat oil in a large skillet over medium-high heat. Add chicken, broccoli, carrots and onion. Cook and stir until broccoli is crisp-tender, about 10 minutes. Add water, bouillon and tarragon; cook and stir until juices run clear when chicken is pierced. Add pasta and cheese. Toss to coat; serve immediately. Serves 4 to 6.

Mary Kelly
Jefferson City, MO

Chicken & Sausage Skilletini

# Chicken & Sausage Skilletini

¼ c. olive oil
2 boneless, skinless chicken
  breasts, cubed
½ lb. spicy ground pork sausage
1 red onion, thinly sliced
2 cloves garlic, minced
14½-oz. can diced tomatoes
1 red pepper, sliced

3 T. brown sugar, packed
1 t. dried basil
½ t. dried oregano
⅛ t. salt
⅛ t. pepper
16-oz pkg. linguine pasta,
  cooked
Optional: fresh oregano leaves

Heat oil in a large skillet over medium heat. Add chicken, sausage, onion and garlic; cook until juices run clear when chicken is pierced. Add tomatoes, red pepper, brown sugar, basil, oregano, salt and pepper; simmer 5 minutes. Add cooked pasta and simmer an additional 5 minutes. Garnish with oregano, if desired. Serves 4 to 6.

Elizabeth Cisneros
Chino Hills, CA

# Potluck Poppy Seed Chicken

*This easy-to-make favorite tastes great!*

4 boneless, skinless chicken
  breasts, cooked and cubed
10¾-oz. can cream of chicken
  soup
8-oz. container sour cream

½ c. butter, melted
1 sleeve round buttery
  crackers, crushed
2 T. poppy seed

Stir together chicken, soup and sour cream in a lightly greased 8"x8" baking pan. Mix butter, crackers and poppy seed; spread mixture over chicken. Bake, uncovered, at 350 degrees for 30 minutes, or until bubbly. Serves 4.

Jennifer Langley
Kannapolis, NC

# Turkey Stroganoff

## toss-ins for a twist

Substitute ground beef or ground chicken for the turkey in this recipe. You can also add a frozen broccoli and carrot mixture for a variation.

7-oz. pkg. medium egg noodles
¾ lb. ground turkey
1 T. olive oil
2 cubes beef bouillon, crumbled
1 T. butter
1 onion, diced
4-oz. can sliced mushrooms, drained
2 cloves garlic, chopped
2 c. sour cream

Cook noodles according to package directions; drain and keep warm. Brown turkey in olive oil in a skillet over medium heat. Add bouillon, stirring well. Remove from heat and set aside. Melt butter in another skillet over medium heat. Sauté onion and mushrooms in melted butter 5 minutes; add garlic, cooking until golden. Add onion mixture to turkey mixture. Stir in sour cream. Heat through; do not boil. Arrange warm noodles on serving plates; spoon stroganoff on top. Serves 2 to 4.

Candi Sparrow
Davie, FL

# BBQ Turkey Meatballs

1 lb. ground turkey
1 onion, minced
1 egg, beaten
½ c. bread crumbs
1 T. milk
1 t. salt
1 c. catsup
1 clove garlic, minced
½ c. brown sugar, packed
¼ c. lemon juice
3 T. Worcestershire sauce
salt and pepper to taste

Combine turkey, onion, egg, bread crumbs, milk and salt in a bowl; mix well. Form into 24 balls; set aside. Add remaining ingredients to a Dutch oven; bring to a boil over medium heat. Add meatballs; cover and simmer about 20 to 25 minutes, until fully cooked. Serves 4.

Paula Lydzinski
Perkasie, PA

# Homemade Turkey Pot Pie

⅓ c. butter
⅓ c. onion, chopped
⅓ c. all-purpose flour
½ t. salt
¼ t. pepper
1¾ c. turkey broth
⅔ c. milk

2½ to 3 c. cooked turkey, chopped
10-oz. pkg. frozen peas and carrots, thawed
14.1-oz. pkg. refrigerated pie crusts

*"This recipe has been in our family for years...a real treat."*
*—Sarah*

Melt butter in a large saucepan over low heat. Stir in onion, flour, salt and pepper. Cook, stirring constantly, until mixture is bubbly; remove from heat. Stir in broth and milk. Heat to boiling, stirring constantly. Boil and stir one minute. Mix in turkey and peas and carrots; set aside. Roll out one pie crust and place in a 9"x9" baking pan. Pour turkey mixture into pan. Roll remaining crust into an 11-inch square; cut out vents with a small cookie cutter. Place crust over filling; turn edges under and crimp. Bake, uncovered, at 425 degrees for 35 minutes, or until golden. Serves 4 to 6.

Sarah Sullivan
Andrews, NC

# Apple-Spice Country Ribs

*One fall weekend after apple picking, I tossed together this recipe. I was trying to work apples into everything I could think of to use them up, and I used some of the last ones in this slow-cooker recipe. Once it was done, I wished I'd made it first so I could make it again!*

## serving suggestion

Instead of rice or noodles, make a barley pilaf. Simply prepare quick-cooking barley with chicken broth seasoned with a little chopped onion and dried parsley. Filling, quick and tasty!

2 to 3 lbs. boneless country pork ribs
3 baking apples, cored and cut into wedges
1 onion, thinly sliced
⅔ c. apple cider

1 t. cinnamon
1 t. allspice
½ t. salt
¼ t. pepper
mashed potatoes or cooked rice

Place all ingredients except potatoes or rice in a 5-quart slow cooker; stir to coat. Cover and cook on low setting for 7 to 9 hours. Juices will thicken as they cool; stir if separated. Serve with mashed potatoes or hot cooked rice. Serves 4 to 6.

Tammi Miller
Attleboro, MA

# Shortcut Stromboli

1 loaf frozen bread dough,
   thawed
1 T. grated Parmesan cheese
2 eggs, separated
2 T. oil
1 t. dried parsley

1 t. dried oregano
½ t. garlic powder
½ lb. deli ham, sliced
¼ lb. deli salami, sliced
6-oz. pkg. shredded Cheddar
   cheese

Spread thawed dough in a rectangle on a greased baking sheet. Mix Parmesan cheese, egg yolks, oil and seasonings in a bowl. Spread Parmesan cheese mixture on top of dough. Layer with meat and Cheddar cheese. Roll up jelly-roll style; place seam-side down on baking sheet. Let rise about 20 minutes. Brush with egg whites. Bake, uncovered, at 350 degrees for 30 to 40 minutes, until golden. Slice to serve. Serves 6.

Becky Kuchenbecker
Ravenna, OH

"I have made this stromboli for family get-togethers, picnics and potlucks, and I've gotten many requests for this quick & easy recipe! You can use different meats and cheeses for a new taste every time."
—Becky

# Farmhands' Stuffed Sandwich

1 round loaf hearty bread
2 T. Italian salad dressing
8 slices provolone cheese, divided
⅛ lb. deli salami, sliced
2¼-oz. can sliced black olives, drained
½ lb. mild Italian pork sausage links, browned and sliced
1 thick slice red onion

6 T. pizza sauce
7 pepperoncini, drained and sliced
¼ lb. deli turkey, sliced
4-oz. jar sun-dried tomatoes in oil, drained and sliced
2 T. shredded Parmesan cheese
Optional: 2 T. garlic, pressed

Slice off top quarter of loaf; hollow out top and bottom of loaf. Brush salad dressing inside bottom half. Layer with half of cheese slices; layer on remaining ingredients in order listed, ending with remaining cheese slices. Replace top half of loaf. Place on an ungreased baking sheet; set another baking sheet on top. Weight with a heavy object such as a food can or a cast-iron skillet. Let stand 30 minutes to one hour. Cut into wedges to serve. Serves 8.

Barbara Shultis
South Egremont, MA

"You'll love this oversized sandwich. Wrapped in plastic, it's perfect for carrying to a picnic. I've done SO many tasty variations on this sandwich...chicken with barbecue sauce, ham & Swiss with coleslaw, corned beef & sauerkraut with Thousand Island dressing. The mix & match possibilities are endless!"

—Barbara

## serving secret

What a clever way to serve a sandwich and chips for lunch...look for jaunty red baskets at restaurant or kitchen supply stores, line with wax paper and serve diner-style!

# Mama's Scrumptious Roast Beef

14-oz. can garlic-seasoned chicken broth
1 c. white wine or chicken broth
3 T. red steak sauce
2 T. brown steak sauce
2 T. balsamic vinegar
2-oz. pkg. onion soup mix

1 T. all-purpose flour
12 to 14 baby carrots
2 red peppers, thinly sliced
2 bunches green onions, chopped
5 to 6 cloves garlic, minced
3- to 4-lb. beef rump roast
salt and pepper to taste

Combine broth, wine or broth, steak sauce, vinegar and soup mix in a large bowl; set aside. Place flour in a large plastic roasting bag; shake bag to coat and arrange in an ungreased roasting pan. Place vegetables and garlic in bag; place roast in bag on top of vegetables. Drizzle broth mixture over roast; season with salt and pepper. Cut 6 one-inch holes in top of roasting bag with a knife tip. Seal bag. Bake at 325 degrees for 3 hours, or until roast is tender. Remove roast to a serving platter; let stand 15 minutes before slicing. Serve vegetables with roast. Serves 6 to 8.

Debbie Donaldson
Andalusia, AL

*"I like to strain the excess liquid from the roasting bag and thicken it with flour to make a flavorful gravy."*

—Debbie

# Marinated Flank Steak

1 to 2 lbs. beef flank steaks
½ c. soy sauce
2 T. honey
2 T. white vinegar
1½ T. ground ginger

1½ t. garlic powder
1½ t. cinnamon
1½ t. nutmeg
¾ c. oil
1 onion, chopped

Make shallow cuts in steaks using a sharp knife; set aside. Mix together remaining ingredients in a large plastic zipping bag; add steaks. Refrigerate for 24 hours, turning several times. Grill or broil for 5 to 10 minutes on each side, or until desired doneness. Slice thinly on an angle to serve. Serves 4 to 6.

Irene Robinson
Cincinnati, OH

# Jalapeño-Bacon Cheese Steak

2 lbs. ground beef chuck
1¾ c. soft bread crumbs
¾ c. beef broth
2 eggs, beaten
1 T. salt
1½ t. pepper
8-oz. pkg. shredded Cheddar
  cheese

8 slices bacon, diced and
  crisply cooked
4 green onions, sliced
2 jalapeño peppers, seeded
  and chopped

## supper in a snap

Serve this with a loaf of buttered bread. Garden-fresh herbs make the best butter. Blend together ½ cup softened butter with ½ cup shredded Cheddar cheese and 3 tablespoons chopped fresh chives. Spread over grilled veggies or rolls, this butter is simply delicious.

Place beef in a large bowl. Mix bread crumbs and broth in a separate bowl until thoroughly combined. Add bread crumb mixture, eggs, salt and pepper to beef; combine gently. Form into 8 patties. Grill over medium heat about 8 minutes on each side, or place on an ungreased baking sheet and bake at 300 degrees for 30 minutes. Top with cheese, bacon, onions and peppers during the last few minutes of cooking. Serves 8.

Lisa Robason
Corpus Christi, TX

# Mushroom + Steak Hoagies

*Soy sauce lends a unique taste to this delicious steak sandwich.*

1 c. water
⅓ c. soy sauce
1½ t. garlic powder
1½ t. pepper
1-lb. round steak, cut into ¼-inch strips
1 onion, sliced
1 green pepper, thinly sliced
4-oz. can mushroom stems and pieces, drained
2 c. shredded mozzarella cheese
6 hoagie buns, split

Whisk together water, soy sauce, garlic powder and pepper in a bowl; add steak, turning to coat. Cover and refrigerate overnight. Drain and discard marinade; brown steak in a large skillet over medium-high heat. Add onion, green pepper and mushrooms; sauté 8 minutes, or until tender. Reduce heat; top with cheese. Remove from heat; stir until cheese melts and meat is coated. Spoon onto buns to serve. Serves 6.

Mandy Sheets
Homedale, ID

# Regina's Stuffed Pitas

½ lb. deli roast beef, cut into thin strips
2 c. romaine lettuce, shredded
1 c. carrots, peeled and shredded
1 c. cucumber, thinly sliced
½ c. red onion, thinly sliced
⅓ c. crumbled feta cheese
3 T. pine nuts, toasted
4 pita rounds, halved and split
2 T. mayonnaise
2 T. milk
1 T. cider vinegar

Stir together beef, vegetables, cheese and nuts. Spoon mixture equally inside pita halves. Whisk together remaining ingredients. Drizzle over pita filling. Serves 4.

Regina Vining
Warwick, RI

Mushroom &
Steak Hoagies

# Mama's Quick Meatball Subs

*"We love our local sub shop's French bread. We often buy day-old loaves for a delicious way to dress up this yummy family treat."*

—Cris

1 lb. extra-lean ground beef
20 saltine crackers, crushed
12-oz. bottle chili sauce, divided
¼ c. grated Parmesan cheese

2 egg whites, beaten
salt and pepper to taste
15-oz. jar pizza sauce, warmed
2 loaves French baguettes, halved and split
2 cups favorite shredded cheese

Combine beef, cracker crumbs, half of chili sauce, Parmesan cheese, egg whites, salt and pepper in a bowl. Mix well; form into 16 (1½-inch) meatballs. Place on a baking sheet sprayed with non-stick vegetable spray. Bake at 400 degrees for 15 minutes, or until golden, turning meatballs halfway through. Add baked meatballs to warmed sauce. Fill each half-loaf with 4 meatballs and sprinkle with cheese. Serve with remaining chili sauce on the side. Serves 4.

Cris Goode
Mooresville, IN

# Aunt Millie's Meatloaf

1 lb. ground beef or
  meatloaf mix
1 to 2 eggs, beaten
1 c. Italian-flavored dry bread
  crumbs
1 onion, diced
1 T. dried parsley
1 T. catsup or tomato sauce
1 t. sugar
1 t. mustard
½ t. dried basil
⅛ t. salt
⅛ t. pepper
⅛ t. garlic powder
1 t. beef bouillon granules
½ c. boiling water

Combine all ingredients except bouillon and boiling water in a large bowl; set aside. Dissolve bouillon in boiling water; add to mixture and mix well. Form into a loaf; place in a greased 9"x5" loaf pan. Bake at 350 degrees for one hour. Serves 4 to 6.

Ida Vasily
Bethlehem, PA

"This recipe has been in our family for over 50 years! It's been a consistently good old-fashioned recipe now serving a fourth generation. Every time I make it, my family raves that it's the best meatloaf they've ever tasted. I know you'll agree once you've made it."

—Ida

# Beefy Onion Bake

1 lb. ground beef
10¾-oz. can cream of
  mushroom soup
10¾-oz. can cream of celery
  soup
10¾-oz. can cream of chicken
  soup
1½-oz. pkg. onion soup mix
2 c. instant rice, uncooked
1½ c. water

Brown beef in a skillet over medium heat until no longer pink; drain. Add remaining ingredients; spread in an ungreased 13"x9" baking pan. Bake, covered, at 325 degrees for 45 minutes, or until hot and bubbly. Serves 8.

Debbie Watson
Maumelle, AR

# Deep-Dish Pizza

1 lb. ground beef
½ c. onion, chopped
2 cloves garlic, minced
2 8½-oz. pkgs. pizza crust mix
14-oz. jar pizza sauce
4-oz. can sliced mushrooms, drained
¼ c. green pepper, chopped
3.8-oz. can sliced black olives, drained
2½ c. shredded mozzarella cheese

Brown beef with onion and garlic in a skillet over medium heat until beef is no longer pink. Drain; set aside. Prepare pizza crust according to package directions. Transfer to a greased 13"x9" baking pan, pressing dough halfway up sides of pan. Pierce dough several times with a fork. Bake at 425 degrees for 5 minutes; remove from oven. Cover with sauce; layer with beef mixture, mushrooms, green pepper, olives and cheese. Bake, uncovered, at 425 degrees for 20 to 25 minutes, until cheese is melted. Serves 6 to 8.

Cris Goode
Mooresville, IN

# Texas Hash
### Sharlene Casteel (Fort Mitchell, AL)

*I got this recipe from someone at church many years ago, and it is still a family favorite...
so easy! Add a side salad, and dinner is ready in a jiffy.*

1 lb. ground beef
1 onion, diced
1 red or green pepper, diced
1 c. long-cooking rice, uncooked
14½-oz. can diced tomatoes

2 c. water
2 t. chili powder
1 t. paprika
salt and pepper to taste
Garnish: fresh thyme sprigs

Brown beef with onion and red or green pepper in a skillet over medium heat; drain. Stir in uncooked rice and remaining ingredients except garnish. Cover and simmer over low heat 25 minutes, or until water is absorbed and rice is tender. Garnish with fresh thyme sprigs. Serves 4 to 6.

# Doreen's Shrimp-Rice Salad

"I've been making this recipe for years... it's simple to make and easily doubled or even tripled."

—Doreen

1 c. long-cooking rice, cooked
1 c. celery, chopped
1 c. green onion, chopped
1 lb. cooked small shrimp
1 c. mayonnaise
1 T. curry powder
8 leaves red leaf lettuce
Optional: slivered almonds, toasted

Combine rice, celery, green onion and shrimp in a large bowl; set aside. Mix together mayonnaise and curry in a small bowl until well blended; stir into rice mixture. Cover and chill at least one hour. Serve over lettuce. Sprinkle with almonds, if desired. Serves 8.

Doreen Matthew
San Marcos, CA

# Herbed Shrimp Tacos

juice of 1 lime
½ c. plus 1 T. fresh cilantro,
  chopped and divided
½ t. salt
½ t. pepper
⅛ t. dried thyme
⅛ t. dried oregano
1 lb. uncooked medium shrimp,
  peeled and cleaned

½ c. radishes, shredded
½ c. cabbage, shredded
½ c. red onion, chopped
Optional: 2 T. oil
10  6-inch flour tortillas,
  warmed
Optional: guacamole, lettuce

Combine lime juice, one tablespoon cilantro, salt, pepper and herbs in a large plastic zipping bag; mix well. Add shrimp; seal bag and refrigerate at least one hour. Combine radishes, cabbage, onion and remaining ½ cup cilantro in a bowl; set aside. Thread shrimp onto skewers; grill over medium-high heat until pink and cooked through, or heat oil in a skillet over medium heat and sauté shrimp until done. Spoon into warm tortillas with cabbage mixture; serve with guacamole and lettuce, if desired. Serves 10.

Lori Vincent
Alpine, UT

# Seafood Pasta Salad

8-oz. pkg. rotini pasta
½ c. mayonnaise-type salad
  dressing
¼ c. Italian salad dressing
2 T. grated Parmesan cheese
1½ c. imitation crabmeat,
  chopped

1 c. frozen broccoli flowerets,
  thawed
½ c. green pepper, chopped
½ c. tomato, chopped
¼ c. green onion, sliced

Cook pasta according to package directions; drain and rinse with cold water. Mix together dressings and Parmesan cheese in a serving bowl. Add pasta and remaining ingredients; toss lightly. Cover and refrigerate at least 2 hours. Serves 4 to 6.

Mary Lou Thomas
Portland, ME

# Eggplant Parmesan

*This is a down-home dish that's great to enjoy with family & friends no matter the occasion. Serve it atop spaghetti noodles.*

2 eggs, beaten
1 T. water
2 eggplants, peeled and sliced
    ¼-inch thick
2 c. Italian-flavored dry bread
    crumbs
1½ c. grated Parmesan cheese,
    divided
27¾-oz. jar garden-style pasta
    sauce, divided
1½ c. shredded mozzarella
    cheese

Combine eggs and water in a shallow bowl. Dip eggplant slices into egg mixture. Arrange slices in a single layer on a greased baking sheet; bake at 350 degrees for 25 minutes, or until golden. Set aside. Mix bread crumbs and ½ cup Parmesan cheese in a bowl; set aside. Spread a small amount of sauce in an ungreased 13"x9" baking pan; layer half the eggplant slices, one cup sauce and one cup bread crumb mixture. Repeat layers. Cover and bake 45 minutes. Uncover; sprinkle with mozzarella cheese and remaining one cup Parmesan cheese. Bake, uncovered, 10 more minutes. Cut into squares. Serves 6 to 8.

Tammy Dillow
Raceland, KY

## toss-ins for a twist

Mix in some provolone with the mozzarella cheese for a delicious flavor.

## crumbs in an instant

Homemade bread crumbs are a snap! Just place Italian bread cubes in a food processor and pulse until the texture becomes fine.

# Santa Fe Grilled Veggie Pizzas

*Make sure to cut the vegetables into equal-size pieces so that they will grill evenly.*

all-purpose flour
10-oz. tube refrigerated pizza crust dough
1 lb. portabella mushrooms, stems removed
1 red pepper, quartered
1 yellow pepper, quartered
1 zucchini, cut lengthwise into ½-inch-thick slices

1 yellow squash, cut lengthwise into ½-inch-thick slices
¾ t. salt
1 c. Alfredo pasta sauce
1¼ c. smoked mozzarella cheese, shredded

Lightly dust 2 baking sheets with flour. On a lightly floured surface, press dough into a 15-inch by 11-inch rectangle. Cut into quarters; place 2 on each baking sheet. Lightly coat vegetables with non-stick vegetable spray; sprinkle with salt. Grill vegetables over medium-high heat about 10 minutes, or until tender. Cut mushrooms and peppers into slices. Cut zucchini and squash in half crosswise. Grill 2 pieces pizza dough at a time over medium heat one minute, or until golden. With tongs, turn dough over and grill 30 more seconds, or until firm. Return to baking sheets. Spread sauce over crusts; top with vegetables and cheese. Grill pizzas, covered, 2 to 3 more minutes, until cheese melts. Serves 4.

April Jacobs
Loveland, CO

*"While waiting for a train in Santa Fe, we stopped for lunch at a little restaurant and ordered grilled vegetable pizza. It was so tasty that I had to find a way to recreate it when we returned home to our ranch in Colorado!"*

*—April*

## grill tricks

When grilling veggies, baste them with a simple marinade that's big on flavor. Whisk together ½ cup melted butter, ½ cup lemon juice and one tablespoon chopped fresh basil.

# Broccoli-Cheddar Soup

1½ c. water
10-oz. pkg. frozen broccoli, thawed
2 T. butter
1 cube chicken bouillon
2 T. dried, minced onion
2¼ c. milk, divided
10¾-oz. can Cheddar cheese soup

1 c. shredded Cheddar cheese
½ t. Worcestershire sauce
⅛ t. salt
⅛ t. pepper
⅛ t. garlic salt
2 T. all-purpose flour
Garnish: additional shredded Cheddar cheese

*"I know I can count on this yummy soup when I want something extra special."*

*—Lisa*

Combine water, broccoli, butter, bouillon cube and onion in a stockpot; cook over medium heat until onion is tender. Add 2 cups milk, soup, cheese, Worcestershire sauce, salt, pepper and garlic salt; cook over low heat until cheese melts. Stir in flour and remaining ¼ cup milk; cook until thickened and heated through. Garnish with additional cheese. Serves 4.

Lisa Peterson
Sabina, OH

Classic Chicken Cacciatore,
page 87

# slow-cooker specials

A slow cooker simmering away means that at the end of the day, a home-cooked meal awaits you! Rediscover family favorites such as Spaghetti for a Crowd and Cheesy Chicken & Potatoes…and make surprising new finds in your slow cooker, such as French Onion Soup. Fall back in love with this time-tested way of cooking!

# Potato-Corn Chowder
Jerry Bostian (Oelwein, IA)

*Short on time? Use a package of ready-cooked bacon instead.*

2 10¾-oz. cans potato soup
2 14¾-oz. cans cream-style corn
8 slices bacon, crisply cooked and
   crumbled, 1 to 2 T. drippings
   reserved

½ to 1 c. milk
salt, pepper and garlic salt to taste
Garnish: fresh parsley, chopped

Blend soup and corn in a 4-quart slow cooker; add bacon along with bacon drippings, if desired. Add milk until soup is of desired consistency; add salt, pepper and garlic salt to taste. Cover and cook on low setting for 8 to 10 hours. Sprinkle individual servings with parsley. Serves 6 to 8.

# French Onion Soup

*Start this soup in the slow cooker after breakfast, and it's ready in time for lunch.*

¼ c. butter
3 c. onion, sliced
1 T. sugar
1 t. salt
2 T. all-purpose flour
4 c. low-sodium beef broth

¼ c. dry white wine or beef broth
6 slices French bread
½ c. grated Parmesan cheese
½ c. shredded mozzarella cheese

Melt butter in a skillet over medium heat. Add onion; cook 15 to 20 minutes, until soft. Stir in sugar and salt; continue to cook and stir until golden. Add flour; mix well. Combine onion mixture, broth and wine or broth in a 4-quart slow cooker. Cover and cook on high setting for 3 to 4 hours. Ladle soup into oven-proof bowls. Top with bread slices; sprinkle with cheeses. Broil until cheese is bubbly and melted. Serves 6.

Robin Hill
Rochester, NY

## slow-cook it

Your favorite stovetop soup, stew or chili recipe can be converted for slow cooking...how convenient! If the soup normally simmers 1½ to 2 hours, just add all the ingredients to the slow cooker and cook on low for 6 to 8 hours.

# Butternut Squash Soup

*Just chop a few ingredients and combine in the slow cooker for a delicious gourmet soup...so easy!*

2½ lbs. butternut squash, peeled, halved, seeded and cubed
2 c. leeks, chopped
2 Granny Smith apples, peeled, cored and diced

2 14½-oz. cans chicken broth
1 c. water
seasoned salt and white pepper to taste
Garnish: sour cream and freshly ground nutmeg

Combine squash, leeks, apples, broth and water in a 4-quart slow cooker. Cover and cook on high setting for 4 hours, or until squash and leeks are tender. Carefully purée the hot soup, in 3 or 4 batches, in a food processor or blender until smooth. Add seasoned salt and white pepper. Garnish with sour cream and nutmeg. Serves 8.

# Spaghetti for a Crowd

*After cooking for several hours, this spaghetti's flavor is tremendous! There's no added oil, so this sauce is low fat, too.*

5 29-oz. cans tomato sauce
3 6-oz. cans tomato paste
1 onion, chopped
3 cloves garlic, minced
3 T. dried rosemary
3 T. dried oregano
3 T. dried thyme

3 T. dried parsley
⅛ t. red pepper flakes
1 bay leaf
8 to 10 c. cooked spaghetti
Garnish: shaved Parmesan
    cheese, fresh thyme sprigs

## toss-ins for a twist

Substitute cooked penne noodles for the spaghetti for a fun change to this traditional favorite.

Combine all ingredients except spaghetti and garnish in a 6-quart slow cooker. Cover and cook on high setting for 3 to 4 hours, stirring frequently. Discard bay leaf. Serve over cooked spaghetti; sprinkle with Parmesan cheese and thyme sprigs. Serves 6 to 10.

# Stewed Chicken Verde

*"This chicken is so tender and juicy... the leftovers make yummy quesadillas, too. I love to use my slow cooker, and I'm always thinking up new ideas to try. This recipe was a hit with my family a couple of years ago, and I've been making it ever since!"*

*—Robin*

3- to 3½-lb. whole chicken
1 T. poultry seasoning
¼ c. onion, sliced
several sprigs fresh cilantro
10¾-oz. can cream of chicken soup
4-oz. can chopped green chiles
cooked rice
Garnish: fresh cilantro sprigs, lime wedges

Sprinkle chicken all over with poultry seasoning. Place onion slices and cilantro sprigs inside chicken. Place chicken in an oval 4-quart slow cooker; top with soup and chiles. Cover and cook on low setting for 7 to 8 hours. Shred the chicken and serve with cooked rice. Garnish with cilantro and lime wedges. Serves 4 to 6.

Robin Acasio
Chula Vista, CA

## size it right

Slow cookers come in so many sizes that you might want to have more than one! A 4-quart size is handy for recipes that will feed about four people, while a 5½- to 6-quart one is terrific for larger families and potluck-size recipes. Just have room for one? Choose an oval slow cooker...roasts and whole chickens will fit perfectly.

# Cheesy Chicken + Potatoes

"I often use my slow cooker at a cabin in Ohio's beautiful Hocking Hills... it allows me to spend more time relaxing with my family. They ask for this recipe every time we go!"
—Barbara

32-oz. pkg. frozen shredded hashbrowns
17-oz. pkg. frozen chopped broccoli
2 10¾-oz. cans Cheddar cheese soup
2 12-oz. cans evaporated milk
1½ lbs. boneless, skinless chicken breasts, cubed
6-oz. can French-fried onions
salt and pepper to taste
12-oz. pkg. shredded Cheddar cheese

Combine hashbrowns, broccoli, soup, milk, chicken and onions in a 5-quart slow cooker sprayed with non-stick vegetable spray. Add salt and pepper to taste; stir well. Cover and cook on high setting for 4 hours or on low setting for 8 to 9 hours. Stir in shredded cheese during the last 30 minutes of cooking time. Serves 6 to 8.

Barbara Cordle
London, OH

# Divine Chicken

6 boneless, skinless chicken breasts
2 10¾-oz. cans cream of chicken soup
1¼ c. milk
3 c. frozen carrots
1½ c. frozen broccoli flowerets
1½-oz. pkg. onion soup mix
3 to 4 c. cooked rice or pasta

Combine all ingredients except rice or pasta in a 4-quart slow cooker. Cover and cook on low setting for 6 to 8 hours. Using a slotted spoon, arrange chicken and vegetables on cooked rice or pasta. Top with sauce from slow cooker. Serves 6.

Wendy Lee Paffenroth
Pine Island, NY

"I created this slow-cooker recipe one morning with the foods I had on hand, and my family loved it!"
—Wendy Lee

## slow-cooker secret

Chicken breasts break apart easily after 5 or more hours of slow cooking on low. Stir gently, breaking up the chicken with a spoon as you stir.

# Company Chicken & Stuffing

*Try Cheddar or brick cheese for a tasty variation in flavor.*

## toss-ins for a twist

If you'd like to add some gravy, purchase a 0.88-oz. package of turkey gravy mix. Prepare it according to package directions, and spoon it onto the stuffing and chicken.

4 boneless, skinless chicken breasts
4 slices Swiss cheese
6-oz. pkg. chicken-flavored stuffing mix
2 10¾-oz. cans cream of chicken soup
½ c. chicken broth

Arrange chicken in a 4-quart slow cooker; top each piece with a slice of cheese. Combine stuffing mix, soup and broth in a bowl; spoon into slow cooker. Cover and cook on low setting for 6 to 8 hours. Serves 4.

Amy Blanchard
Hazel Park, MI

# Classic Chicken Cacciatore

*Also try this rich, saucy stew served over rice or thin spaghetti.*

2 T. olive oil
2 boneless, skinless chicken
  breasts, cut into strips
½ c. all-purpose flour
pepper to taste
½ c. white wine or chicken
  broth, divided
1 onion, chopped
1 green pepper, chopped
2 cloves garlic, minced
2 T. fresh Italian parsley,
  chopped

½ t. dried oregano
½ t. dried basil
14-oz. can diced Italian
  tomatoes
14-oz. jar Italian pasta sauce
  with vegetables
8-oz. pkg. mushrooms,
  chopped
6-oz. pkg. penne pasta,
  cooked
Garnish: grated Parmesan
  cheese

Heat oil in a skillet over medium heat. Coat chicken in flour and sprinkle with pepper; brown in skillet 3 to 5 minutes on each side. Place chicken in a 5-quart slow cooker on high setting. Stir in ¼ cup wine or broth. Add onion, green pepper, garlic and herbs; cover and cook until onion is tender. Add tomatoes, pasta sauce, mushrooms and remaining ¼ cup wine or broth; cover and cook to a slow boil, about 30 minutes to one hour. Serve over cooked noodles; sprinkle with Parmesan cheese. Serves 3 to 4.

Jackie Smulski
Lyons, IL

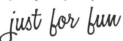

## just for fun

Create a cozy Italian restaurant feel for your next pasta dinner. Toss a red & white checked tablecloth over the table, light drip candles in empty bottles and add a basket of garlic bread.

# Creamy Chicken + Asparagus

4 boneless, skinless chicken breasts
10¾-oz. can cream of chicken soup
2 c. milk
pepper to taste
dried, minced onion to taste
2 to 4 slices pasteurized process cheese spread, diced
1 lb. fresh asparagus, trimmed and cut into 1-inch pieces
3 to 4 c. cooked rice

## toss-ins for a twist

Substitute broccoli for the asparagus, if you like.

Arrange chicken in a 4-quart slow cooker. Combine soup, milk, pepper, onion and cheese in a bowl; pour over chicken. Cover and cook on low setting for 7 hours. Add asparagus; increase heat to high setting. Cover and cook for one hour, or until asparagus is crisp-tender. Serve over cooked rice. Serves 4.

Ellen Lockhart
Blacksburg, VA

## make it special

Look for distinctive platters, bowls or even a whole set of special dishes to use on holidays and birthdays with your family. Years from now, your children and grand-children will cherish these dishes for the memories they bring back.

# Chicken + Rice Soup with Mushrooms

## supper in a snap

Use a rotisserie chicken for convenience. The average chicken will yield about 3 cups of chopped cooked meat.

1 T. olive oil
1 c. onion, chopped
½ c. celery, chopped
8-oz. pkg. sliced mushrooms
2 cloves garlic, minced
2 c. water
5 c. chicken broth

3 c. cooked chicken, chopped
2 T. fresh parsley, chopped
1 t. chicken bouillon granules
6-oz. pkg. long-grain and wild rice mix

Heat oil in a large skillet over medium-high heat. Add onion, celery, mushrooms and garlic. Sauté 4 minutes, or until vegetables are tender; add 2 cups water, stirring to loosen particles from bottom of skillet. Combine vegetable mixture, broth and remaining ingredients (including seasoning packet from rice mix) in a 4- or 5-quart slow cooker. Cover and cook on low setting 4 to 4½ hours, until rice is tender. Serves 8.

# Beef Tips + Noodles

3- to 4-lb. beef chuck roast, cubed
salt and pepper to taste
10¾-oz. can golden mushroom soup
10¾-oz. can cream of mushroom soup
2½ c. water
0.53-oz. pkg. French onion soup mix
2 T. all-purpose flour
3 T. cold water
8-oz. container sour cream
8-oz. pkg. medium egg noodles, cooked

Season beef with salt and pepper; place in a 6-quart slow cooker. Stir together soups, 2½ cups water and soup mix in a bowl; add to slow cooker. Cover and cook on high for 6 to 7 hours, until beef is tender. Stir flour into 3 tablespoons cold water in a small bowl; add to slow cooker, stirring gently. Cover and cook on high about 15 minutes, or until gravy is desired consistency. Stir in sour cream. Serve over cooked noodles. Serves 6.

Suzette Rummell
Cuyahoga Falls, OH

"This is my daughter's favorite dinner when she comes home from college. She always lets me know to put it on the menu before she arrives. We like to use Amish-made egg noodles."
—Suzette

# Swiss Steak
Lisa Ludwig (Fort Wayne, IN)

2-lb. beef chuck roast, cut into
  serving-size pieces
¾ c. all-purpose flour, divided
2 to 3 T. oil
14½-oz. can diced tomatoes
1 onion, sliced

1 red pepper, sliced
1 stalk celery, chopped
1 T. browning and seasoning
  sauce
mashed potatoes or cooked rice

Coat beef with ½ cup flour; sauté in oil in a skillet over medium heat until browned on all sides. Arrange beef in a 5-quart slow cooker. Combine tomatoes, onion, pepper, celery and sauce in a bowl; pour over beef. Cover and cook on low setting for 6 to 8 hours. Slowly stir in remaining ¼ cup flour to make gravy, adding water if necessary. Cover and cook on high setting for 15 minutes, or until thickened. Serve over mashed potatoes or hot cooked rice. Serves 4.

# Fajitas

*These are always a favorite for casual dinner parties or when the whole family gets together...and the slow cooker does all the work!*

1½ lbs. beef round steak
14½-oz. can diced tomatoes, drained
1 onion, sliced
1 green pepper, cut into strips
1 red pepper, cut into strips
1 jalapeño pepper, chopped
2 cloves garlic, minced
1 t. chili powder

1 t. ground cumin
1 t. ground coriander
1 t. fresh cilantro, chopped
¼ t. salt
8 to 10 flour tortillas
Garnish: sour cream, guacamole, salsa, shredded cheese, shredded lettuce, fresh cilantro

Place beef in the bottom of a 4-quart slow cooker. Combine remaining ingredients except tortillas and garnish in a bowl; spoon over beef. Cover and cook on high setting for 4 to 5 hours or on low setting for 8 to 10 hours. Shred beef; stir into mixture in slow cooker. Serve with a slotted spoon on tortillas and garnish with favorite toppings. Serves 8 to 10.

Erin Gunn
Omaha, NE

## when company comes

A tray of warm, moistened towels will be welcomed by your guests after a meal of finger foods. Soak fingertip towels in water and a bit of lemon juice, roll up and microwave on high 10 to 15 seconds.

# Lillian's Beef Stew

*"My mother made this for us when we were small children, and now I make it for my own family. It's a wonderful dinner to come home to on a cold day."*

*—Nancy*

2 lbs. stew beef cubes
2 potatoes, peeled and quartered
3 stalks celery, diced
4 carrots, peeled and cut into thick slices
2 onions, quartered
2 c. cocktail vegetable juice
⅓ c. quick-cooking tapioca, uncooked
1 T. sugar
1 T. salt
½ t. dried basil
¼ t. pepper

Arrange beef and vegetables in a 4-quart slow cooker. Combine remaining ingredients in a bowl; pour into slow cooker. Cover and cook on low setting for 8 to 10 hours. Serves 8.

Nancy Dynes
Goose Creek, SC

## quick beer bread

Stir up a loaf of beer bread for dinner. Combine 2 cups self-rising flour, a 12-ounce can of beer and 3 tablespoons sugar in a greased loaf pan. Bake at 350 degrees for 25 minutes, and drizzle with melted butter. Fragrant and tasty!

# Spanish Rice

*Corn chips are tasty for scooping up this delicious dish.*

2 lbs. ground beef, browned
   and drained
28-oz. can crushed tomatoes
8-oz. can tomato sauce
2 green peppers, chopped
2 onions, chopped

1 c. water
2½ t. chili powder
2 t. salt
2 t. Worcestershire sauce
1 c. long-cooking rice,
   uncooked

Combine all ingredients in a 5-quart slow cooker; mix well. Cover and cook on high setting for 3½ hours or on low setting for 6 to 8 hours. Serves 8 to 10.

Sharon Crider
Lebanon, MO

## The Best Pot Roast Ever

*This roast cooks up so tender...you'll love the gravy, too.*

2 c. water
5 to 6-lb. beef pot roast
1-oz. pkg. ranch salad
  dressing mix
0.7-oz. pkg. Italian salad
  dressing mix

0.87-oz. pkg. brown gravy mix
6 to 8 potatoes, peeled and cut
  into 1-inch pieces
8 to 10 carrots, peeled and
  sliced

Pour 2 cups water into a 7-quart slow cooker; add roast. Combine mixes in a small bowl; sprinkle over roast. Cover and cook on low setting for 6 to 7 hours; add potatoes and carrots during the last 2 hours of cooking. Serves 6 to 8.

Joan Brochu
Hardwick, VT

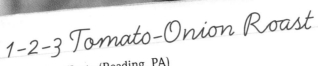

# 1-2-3 Tomato-Onion Roast

Jacqueline Kurtz (Reading, PA)

*This is so delicious that you won't believe how simple it is!*

3 to 4-lb. beef chuck roast
1½-oz. pkg. onion soup mix
14½-oz. can stewed tomatoes,
   undrained

cooked rice

Place roast in a 4-quart slow cooker; top with soup mix and tomatoes. Cover and cook on low setting for 8 hours. Serve over hot cooked rice. Serves 6 to 8.

## Fix + Forget Stuffed Peppers

*Use red or yellow peppers for bright color and a milder taste.*

1½ lbs. ground beef
1 c. long-cooking rice, uncooked
1 onion, chopped
1 carrot, peeled and shredded
1 t. beef bouillon granules
½ t. salt
½ t. pepper
6 yellow, orange or red peppers, tops and seeds removed
10¾-oz. can tomato soup
1¼ c. water

Combine beef, rice, onion, carrot, bouillon, salt and pepper in a bowl; stuff each pepper about two-thirds full with beef mixture. Arrange peppers side by side in a 5-quart slow cooker. Combine soup and 1¼ cups water in a bowl; pour over peppers. Cover and cook on low setting for 6 to 8 hours. Serves 6.

Beth Kramer
Port Saint Lucie, FL

### supper in a snap

With work, school and after-school activities, preparing dinner can be a challenge. Now's the time to get out that slow cooker! Other than chopping a few ingredients, recipes are usually a simple matter of tossing everything into the pot.

## 3-Meat Slow-Cooker Chili

1 lb. ground beef, browned and drained
1 lb. ground sausage, browned and drained
1 lb. bacon, crisply cooked and crumbled
4 15-oz. cans tomato sauce
3 16-oz. cans kidney beans, drained and rinsed
2 T. chili seasoning
15¼-oz. can corn, drained

Place beef, sausage and bacon in a greased 6-quart slow cooker; stir in tomato sauce, beans and seasoning. Cover and cook on low setting 4 to 6 hours; add corn during last hour. Makes 13½ cups.

Beth Goblirsch
Minneapolis, MN

Vegetable-Beef Soup

# Vegetable-Beef Soup

*This recipe is as tasty as it is easy...it also freezes well.*

1 lb. ground beef, browned
 and drained
16-oz. pkg. frozen mixed
 vegetables
11½-oz. can cocktail vegetable
 juice

3 c. water
½ c. pearled barley
1-oz. pkg. onion soup mix
3 cubes beef bouillon
Garnish: sour cream,
 fresh parsley

Combine all ingredients except garnish in a 5-quart slow cooker. Cover and cook on low setting for 6 to 8 hours. Garnish, if desired. Serves 4 to 6.

Cami Cherryholmes
Urbana, IA

## toss-ins for a twist

This is a great way to use whatever vegetables you have on hand. Most types of vegetables will work well in this soup.

# Slow-Cooker Pizza

*This is a great dish for any potluck gathering!*

½ lb. ground beef
1 onion, chopped
16-oz. jar pizza sauce
8-oz. jar spaghetti sauce
12-oz. pkg. kluski egg noodles,
 cooked

8-oz. pkg. sliced pepperoni
8-oz. pkg. shredded mozzarella
 cheese
8-oz. pkg. shredded Cheddar
 cheese

Brown beef and onion in a large skillet over medium heat; drain. Stir in sauces; simmer until heated through. Layer half the noodles in a 5-quart slow cooker and top with half each of meat sauce, pepperoni and cheeses. Repeat layering. Cover and cook on high setting for 30 minutes or on low setting for one hour, until cheese is melted. Serves 8 to 10.

Amanda Rickelman
Pulaski, IA

# Slow-Cooker Steak Chili

## supper in a snap

Freeze this chili in a plastic zipping bag for up to one month for a quick weeknight supper. Thaw the frozen chili in the refrigerator overnight. Then microwave at high for 6 to 7 minutes, until bubbly, stirring after 3 minutes.

2 lbs. beef round steak, cut into 1-inch cubes
1½ c. onion, chopped
2 cloves garlic, minced
2 T. oil
1⅓ c. water, divided
2  15-oz. cans kidney beans, drained and rinsed
2  14½-oz. cans diced tomatoes
16-oz. jar salsa
15-oz. can tomato sauce
1 c. celery, chopped
1½ T. chili powder
1 t. ground cumin
1 t. dried oregano
½ t. pepper
2 T. all-purpose flour
2 T. cornmeal
Garnish: shredded Cheddar cheese, sour cream, crushed tortilla chips

Brown beef, onion and garlic in oil in a large skillet over medium heat; drain. Add beef mixture to a 5-quart slow cooker. Stir in one cup water and remaining ingredients except flour, cornmeal and garnish; mix well. Cover and cook on low setting for 8 hours. Combine flour, cornmeal and remaining ⅓ cup water in a small bowl, whisking until smooth. Add mixture to simmering chili right before serving; stir 2 minutes, or until thickened. Garnish as desired. Serves 8.

Mignonne Gardner
Pleasant Grove, UT

## rinse it away

Drain and rinse canned beans before using…you'll be washing away any "tinny" taste. The added bonus is that you'll reduce the sodium content as well.

# 6-Bean Casserole

"I remember my mom making this hearty slow-cooker dish for large gatherings when I was a child. It was my favorite then and still is today, especially after a few small additions."

—Andrea

1 lb. ground beef, browned and drained
½ lb. bacon, crisply cooked and crumbled
16-oz. can light red kidney beans
15-oz. can green beans
15-oz. can yellow wax beans
15-oz. can butter beans
15-oz. can Great Northern beans

16-oz. can pork & beans, undrained
½ c. onion, chopped
½ c. catsup
1 T. brown sugar, packed
1 T. dry mustard
1 t. sugar
1 t. salt
2 t. white vinegar

Lightly grease the top edge of a 5-quart slow cooker. Add beef and bacon to slow cooker; set aside. Drain all beans except pork & beans; place in a large bowl. Add undrained pork & beans to bowl; stir gently and add to beef mixture in slow cooker. Combine remaining ingredients in a small bowl; add to slow cooker and stir gently. Cover and cook on high setting for 2 to 3 hours. Serves 8 to 10.

Andrea Royer-James
Indiana, PA

# Ham + Potato Soup

3½ c. potatoes, peeled and diced
3¼ c. water
⅓ c. celery, chopped
⅓ c. onion, finely chopped
¾ c. cooked ham, diced
6 cubes chicken bouillon

1 t. pepper
½ t. salt
5 T. butter
5 T. all-purpose flour
2 c. milk
Garnish: celery leaves

## toss-ins for a twist

Top this soup with chives or chopped green onions and Cheddar cheese for added flavor.

Combine all ingredients except butter, flour and milk in a 5-quart slow cooker. Cover and cook on low setting for 6 to 8 hours, or until potatoes are fork-tender. About 20 minutes before serving, melt butter in a saucepan over medium heat; stir in flour. Gradually add milk, stirring constantly until thickened. Stir mixture into soup in slow cooker. Cover and cook on low setting 15 to 20 more minutes, until thickened. Garnish, if desired. Serves 8.

Tiffany Burdette
Everson, WA

# Easy Pork & Sauerkraut

*So tasty! This recipe is very easy to double for heartier appetites.*

1 lb. boneless pork, cubed
32-oz. jar sauerkraut, drained
12-oz. bottle beer
½ apple, peeled and cored

1 T. garlic, minced
2 t. dill weed
1 t. onion salt
1 t. dry mustard

Combine all ingredients in a 4-quart slow cooker; cover and cook on high setting for one hour. Reduce heat to low setting and cook for 5 hours, or until pork is cooked through. Discard apple before serving. Serves 4 to 6.

Carrie Knotts
Kalispell, MT

# Smoky Sausage Dinner

*For even simpler preparation, use canned small potatoes and cook just until everything is heated through.*

1 lb. smoked sausage, cut
   into 1-inch pieces
6 to 8 potatoes, peeled and
   quartered

2 14½-oz. cans French-style
   green beans, drained and
   juice of 1 can reserved
salt and garlic powder to taste

Brown sausage; drain. Arrange potatoes in a 5-quart slow cooker; top with green beans and reserved juice. Arrange sausage on top; sprinkle with salt and garlic powder. Cover and cook on high setting about 6 hours, until potatoes are tender. Serves 4 to 6.

Lisa Hains
Tipp City, OH

## supper in a snap

Prepare everything for this dish the night before and refrigerate in the slow-cooker removable insert. Then simply turn on the slow cooker in the morning before you walk out the door to come home to a delicious home-cooked meal.

Smoky Sausage Dinner

# Down-Home Split Pea Soup

Jude Trimnal (Brevard, NC)

*Let this comfort-food favorite simmer in the slow cooker all afternoon.*

8 c. water
2 c. dried split peas, sorted and
   rinsed
1½ c. celery, sliced
1½ c. carrots, peeled and sliced

1 onion, sliced
2 bay leaves
salt and pepper to taste
1 to 2 c. cooked ham, cubed

Combine all ingredients in a 4-quart slow cooker. Cover and cook on low setting for 4 to 6 hours. Discard bay leaves before serving. Serves 8 to 10.

# Creamy Crab + Shrimp Bisque

1 lb. cooked crabmeat, chopped
½ lb. cooked shrimp, chopped
10¾-oz. can cream of celery soup
10¾-oz. can cream of potato soup
10¾-oz. can cream of asparagus soup
2 c. half-and-half
2 c. milk
¼ c. butter
seafood seasoning to taste

Combine all ingredients in a large slow cooker. Cover and cook on low setting for 3 to 4 hours. Serves 6 to 8.

Barbara Ferree
New Freedom, PA

"This is one of the easiest and tastiest cream soup recipes I have ever tried. It always brings rave reviews, and people cannot believe how simple it is to put together in the slow cooker!"

—Barbara

## party perfect

This rich and creamy soup is perfect for a party because you can keep it warm in the slow cooker while you mingle with your guests. Serve the bisque with mixed salad greens and crusty French bread.

Sourdough Chicken
Casserole, page 120

# one-dish favorites

Getting a homestyle supper to the table fast is a priority for families on the go, and these meal-in-one recipes make dinnertime much easier. Serve up hearty Chicken Spaghetti Deluxe or Aztec Casserole. Don't forget comforting favorites such as Chicken-Zucchini Casserole. The family will come running to the table for these tasty choices.

# Easy Chicken & Couscous

1¼ c. water
¼ c. olive oil, divided
5.8-oz. pkg. chicken-flavored couscous, uncooked
½ c. red pepper, chopped
3 T. onion, chopped
2 cloves garlic, minced
2 c. cooked chicken, cubed
6-oz. jar marinated artichoke hearts, drained and chopped
3.8-oz. can sliced black olives, drained
4-oz. container crumbled feta cheese

Bring water and 2 tablespoons oil to a boil in a saucepan over high heat; add seasoning packet from couscous package, red pepper, onion and garlic. Boil 2 to 3 minutes. Add couscous and cook according to package directions. Remove from heat; cover and let stand 5 minutes, or until all liquid is absorbed. Fluff with a fork. Toss chicken, artichokes and olives in a large serving bowl. Stir in couscous mixture. Add remaining 2 tablespoons oil; mix well. Sprinkle with feta cheese. Serves 4 to 6.

Mary Rose Kulczak
Noblesville, IN

# Chicken, Lime + Tortilla Soup

3 to 3½ lbs. chicken
2 tomatoes, chopped
1 jalapeño pepper, chopped
¼ c. fresh cilantro, chopped
juice of 3 limes
2 t. Worcestershire sauce
1 onion, chopped
½ c. red pepper, chopped
¼ c. corn

¼ c. long-cooking rice,
  uncooked
1 t. chopped green chiles
1 t. garlic, minced
½ t. pepper
salt to taste
Garnish: diced avocado,
  shredded Mexican blend
  cheese, tortilla strips

Cover chicken with water in a stockpot. Bring to a boil over medium-high heat. Reduce heat to low; simmer about an hour, or until chicken is very tender and juices run clear when pierced. Remove chicken to a plate, reserving 4 cups broth in stockpot. Let chicken cool slightly. Add tomatoes, jalapeño, cilantro, lime juice and Worcestershire sauce to reserved broth; simmer 45 minutes. Meanwhile, chop half the chicken and set aside; reserve the rest for another recipe. Stir remaining ingredients except garnish into soup; simmer 20 more minutes. Stir in chopped chicken. Garnish individual servings as desired. Serves 6.

Lisa Lankins
Mazatlan, Mexico

# Creamy Chicken Casserole

32-oz. pkg. onion-flavored
  frozen potato puffs
4 to 6 boneless, skinless
  chicken breasts

10¾-oz. can cream of
  mushroom soup

Place potato puffs in a 4- or 5-quart slow cooker. Place chicken breasts on top; and pour soup over all. Cover and cook on high setting for 4 to 6 hours or on low setting for 8 to 10 hours. Serves 4 to 6.

Jennifer Vander Meersch
Rock Island, IL

*"This is such a delicious soup. I hope you'll try it! I've been making it for ages, and since I moved here several years ago, it has taken on the real flavors of Mexico. I've made a few changes to make it easier for everyone 'up north.'"*

—Lisa

Chicken Spaghetti
Deluxe

# Chicken Spaghetti Deluxe

2 c. cooked chicken, chopped
8-oz. pkg. spaghetti, uncooked
  and broken into 2-inch pieces
1 c. celery, chopped
1 c. onion, chopped
1 c. yellow pepper, chopped
1 c. red pepper, chopped

2 10¾-oz. cans cream of
  mushroom soup
1 c. chicken broth
¼ t. Cajun seasoning or
  pepper
1 c. shredded Cheddar cheese

Mix chicken, spaghetti, celery, onion, yellow pepper and red pepper in a bowl. Whisk together soup, broth and seasoning in a separate bowl. Add chicken mixture. Spread chicken mixture in a lightly greased 13"x9" baking pan; sprinkle cheese over top. Cover with aluminum foil coated with non-stick vegetable spray. Bake at 350 degrees for 45 minutes. Uncover and bake 10 more minutes. Serves 8.

*"This recipe is reminiscent of cold winter days and the inviting smells of Mom's warm kitchen. Best of all, the pasta doesn't need to be cooked ahead of time."*
—Dorothy

Dorothy Benson
Baton Rouge, LA

# Chicken Chimmies

2 boneless, skinless chicken
  breasts, cooked and shredded
salt, pepper and garlic salt,
  to taste
1 T. butter
10 8-inch flour tortillas

8-oz. pkg. shredded Monterey
  Jack cheese
6 green onions, diced
1 T. vegetable oil
Toppings: sour cream,
  guacamole, salsa
Optional: lettuce leaves

Sprinkle chicken with salt, pepper and garlic salt to taste. Heat butter in a large skillet over medium heat; add chicken and sauté about 3 minutes. Spoon chicken evenly onto tortillas. Top with cheese and green onions; fold sides up and roll up, burrito-style. Heat oil in a large skillet over medium-high heat. Add rolled up tortillas and sauté 3 to 6 minutes, until golden. Serve with your choice of toppings and over lettuce leaves, if desired. Serves 6 to 8.

Diana Duff
Cypress, CA

# Top-Prize Chicken Casserole

"This crowd-pleasing dish has graced my family's table for decades. With its creamy sauce and crunchy topping, it's always a hit."

—Betty Lou

2 to 3 c. cooked chicken, cubed
2 10¾-oz. cans cream of mushroom soup
4 eggs, hard-boiled, peeled and chopped
1 onion, chopped
2 c. cooked rice
1½ c. celery, chopped
1 c. mayonnaise
2 T. lemon juice
3-oz. pkg. slivered almonds
5-oz. can chow mein noodles

Combine all ingredients except almonds and noodles in a large bowl; mix well. Place chicken mixture in a lightly greased 3-quart casserole dish. Cover and refrigerate 8 hours to overnight. Stir in almonds. Bake, uncovered, at 350 degrees for 40 to 45 minutes, until heated through. Top with noodles; bake 5 more minutes. Serves 6 to 8.

Betty Lou Wright
Hendersonville, TN

# Chicken Tetrazzini

12-oz. pkg. fettuccine pasta, uncooked
7 T. butter, divided
1 c. sliced mushrooms
½ c. onion, chopped
¼ c. all-purpose flour
1 t. salt
¼ t. pepper
2 c. half-and-half
¼ c. chicken broth
2 c. cooked chicken, chopped
⅓ c. grated Parmesan cheese
1 c. dry bread crumbs

Prepare pasta according to package directions; drain. Melt one tablespoon butter in a skillet over medium heat. Sauté mushrooms and onion in butter until golden; remove from skillet. Melt ¼ cup butter in same skillet; whisk in flour, salt and pepper, stirring until smooth and bubbly. Add half-and-half; boil one minute. Remove from heat; stir in broth, chicken, fettuccine and mushroom mixture. Spoon into a greased 13"x9" baking pan. Sprinkle with Parmesan cheese; set aside. Melt remaining 2 tablespoons butter and toss with bread crumbs; spread over casserole. Bake, uncovered, at 350 degrees for 35 to 45 minutes. Serves 6.

# Spicy Sausage & Chicken Creole

14½-oz. can chopped tomatoes
½ c. long-cooking rice, uncooked
½ c. hot water
2 t. hot pepper sauce
¼ t. garlic powder
¼ t. dried oregano
16-oz. pkg. frozen broccoli, corn & red pepper blend, thawed
4 boneless, skinless chicken thighs
½ lb. Italian sausage links, cooked and quartered
8-oz. can tomato sauce

Combine tomatoes, rice, water, hot sauce and seasonings in an ungreased 13"x9" baking pan. Cover and bake at 375 degrees for 10 minutes. Stir vegetables into tomato mixture; top with chicken and sausage. Pour tomato sauce over top. Bake, covered, at 375 degrees for 40 minutes, or until juices run clear when chicken is pierced. Serves 4.

Carrie Knotts
Kalispell, MT

Make-Ahead
Chicken-Chile Rolls

# Make-Ahead Chicken-Chile Rolls

6 boneless, skinless chicken
  breasts
¼ lb. Monterey Jack cheese,
  cut into 6 strips
7-oz. can diced green chiles
½ c. dry bread crumbs
½ c. grated Parmesan cheese
1 T. chili powder
½ t. salt
¼ t. pepper
¼ t. ground cumin
6 T. butter, melted
2 c. enchilada sauce
Garnish: shredded Mexican
  blend cheese, diced
  tomatoes, chopped
  green onions

### toss-ins for a twist

If your family prefers spicy
dishes, add some Monterey
Jack cheese with jalapeño
peppers for an added kick.

Flatten chicken breasts to ¼-inch thickness between pieces of wax paper. Top each piece of chicken with one strip of cheese and 2 tablespoons chiles; roll up. Combine bread crumbs, Parmesan cheese and seasonings in a bowl; place melted butter in a separate bowl. Dip chicken rolls in butter and coat in crumb mixture. Arrange chicken rolls in a lightly greased 13"x9" baking pan, seam-side down; drizzle with any remaining butter. Cover and chill overnight. The next day, uncover and bake at 400 degrees for 30 minutes, or until heated through. Shortly before serving time, warm enchilada sauce in a saucepan or in the microwave; ladle sauce evenly over chicken. Garnish as desired. Serves 6.

# Pixie's Chicken Casserole

4 c. cooked chicken, cubed
2 c. celery, diced
2 10¾-oz. cans cream of
  chicken soup
1½ c. mayonnaise
2 c. cooked rice
1 T. dried, minced onion
salt and pepper to taste
1 c. cashew halves
2 c. chow mein noodles

Combine all ingredients except cashews and noodles in a lightly greased 13"x9" baking pan. Top with cashews and noodles; bake, uncovered, at 375 degrees for 40 minutes. Serves 6 to 8.

Kelly Elliot
Burns, TN

# Cornbread + Chicken Pie

2 c. cooked chicken, diced
11-oz. can corn, drained
10¾-oz. can cream of
  mushroom soup
10¾-oz. can cream of
  broccoli soup

7-oz. pkg. corn muffin mix
1 egg, beaten
⅓ c. milk
Garnish: shredded Cheddar
  cheese

Combine chicken, corn and soups in a lightly greased 9"x9" baking pan; smooth mixture with a spoon. Stir corn muffin mix, egg and milk in a separate bowl just until moistened; pour over chicken mixture. Bake, uncovered, at 350 degrees for 30 to 35 minutes, until cornbread topping is golden. Garnish with cheese. Serves 6.

Kristina Stewart
Waxahachie, TX

## toss-ins for a twist

Add a can of green chiles for a spicy kick!

# Sourdough Chicken Casserole

4 c. sourdough bread, cubed
6 T. butter, melted and divided
⅓ c. grated Parmesan cheese
2 T. fresh parsley, chopped
2 sweet onions, sliced
8-oz. pkg. sliced mushrooms
10¾-oz. can cream of
  mushroom soup

1 c. white wine or buttermilk
2½ c. cooked chicken, shredded
½ c. roasted red peppers,
  drained and chopped
½ t. salt
¼ t. pepper

"My husband really enjoys this delicious dish, and he's not a big fan of chicken. The caramelized onions give it a great flavor!"

—Brenda

Toss together bread cubes, ¼ cup butter, cheese and parsley in a large bowl; set aside. Sauté onions in remaining 2 tablespoons butter in a large skillet over medium-high heat 15 minutes, or until dark golden. Add mushrooms and sauté 5 minutes. Add remaining ingredients. Cook 5 more minutes, stirring constantly, until hot and bubbly. Pour into 4 lightly greased ramekins; top each ramekin with bread cube mixture. Bake, uncovered, at 400 degrees for 15 minutes, or until golden. Serves 4.

Brenda Hager
Nancy, KY

Sourdough Chicken Casserole

# Greek Chicken + Rice Soup

*When you serve a rotisserie chicken with rice for supper, reserve some to enjoy in soup for the next night. Pita bread and tomatoes pair well with this soup.*

4 c. **chicken broth**
2 c. **cooked rice**
2 **egg yolks**, beaten
1 T. **lemon zest**
3 T. **lemon juice**
1 to 2 c. **deli roast chicken**, shredded

**salt** and **pepper** to taste
Optional: 2 T. **fresh dill** or **parsley**, chopped
Garnish: **sliced black olives, lemon slices**

Bring broth to a simmer in a large saucepan over medium heat. Transfer one cup hot broth to a blender. Add ½ cup cooked rice, egg yolks, lemon zest and juice to blender; cover and blend until smooth. Stir rice mixture into simmering broth; add chicken and remaining rice. Simmer, stirring frequently, about 10 minutes, until slightly thickened. Add salt and pepper to taste. At serving time, stir in dill or parsley, and garnish, if desired. Serves 4.

Dawn Henning
Gooseberry Patch

## supper in a snap

For a speedy Greek salad that can be made any time of year, combine quartered roma tomatoes with sliced black olives, crumbled feta cheese and chopped red onion. Drizzle with Italian salad dressing and toss to mix.

# Fluffy Chicken + Dumplings

*This is a wonderful way to warm up on a chilly night!*

1 to 2 T. vegetable oil
1 c. celery, chopped
1 c. carrots, peeled and sliced
1 T. onion, chopped
49-oz. can chicken broth
10¾-oz. can cream of chicken
   soup

⅛ t. pepper
2 c. cooked chicken, chopped
1⅔ c. biscuit baking mix
⅔ c. milk
Garnish: chopped fresh parsley

Heat oil in a Dutch oven over medium-high heat; sauté celery, carrots and onion 7 minutes, or until crisp-tender. Add broth, soup and pepper; bring to a boil. Reduce heat to low; stir in chicken and continue to simmer. Stir together baking mix and milk to make dumplings in a bowl. Drop by large spoonfuls into simmering broth. Cover and cook on low heat 15 minutes without lifting the lid to allow dumplings to cook. Garnish, if desired. Serves 6.

Angela Lengacher
Montgomery, IN

## supper in a snap

A jar of dried, minced onion can be a real time-saver! If the recipe has a lot of liquid, as in a soup or stew, use it in place of fresh onions. Just substitute one tablespoon of dried, minced onion for every ⅓ cup diced fresh onion.

# Creamy White Chicken Chili

## supper in a snap

This makes a great busy week-night family dinner. Serve it with tortilla chips and toppings such as sour cream, shredded cheese and guacamole. Mexican cornbread would also pair nicely with this dish.

1 lb. boneless, skinless chicken, cubed
1 onion, chopped
1½ t. garlic powder
1 T. oil
2 15½-oz. cans Great Northern beans, drained and rinsed
14½-oz. can chicken broth
2 4-oz. cans green chiles
1 t. salt
1 t. ground cumin
1 t. dried oregano
½ t. pepper
¼ t. cayenne pepper
8-oz. container sour cream
½ c. whipping cream

Sauté chicken, onion and garlic powder in oil in a large saucepan over medium heat until juices run clear when chicken is pierced. Add beans, broth, chiles and seasonings; bring to a boil. Reduce heat; simmer, uncovered, 30 minutes. Remove from heat; stir in sour cream and whipping cream. Serve immediately. Serves 8.

Mary Van Peursem
Kasson, MN

# Zesty Roasted Chicken and Potatoes

6 boneless, skinless chicken breasts
1 lb. redskin potatoes, quartered
⅓ c. mayonnaise
3 T. Dijon mustard
½ t. pepper
2 cloves garlic, pressed
Optional: chopped fresh chives

Arrange chicken and potatoes in a lightly greased 15"x10" jelly-roll pan. Blend remaining ingredients except chives; brush over chicken and potatoes. Bake, uncovered, at 350 degrees for 30 to 35 minutes or until potatoes are tender and juices of chicken run clear when pierced. Sprinkle with chives, if desired, before serving. Serves 6.

Denise Mainville
Mesa, AZ

# Layered Tortilla Pie

1 lb. boneless chicken or beef,
  cut into strips
1 to 2 t. oil
1 c. enchilada sauce
1 t. chili powder
½ t. ground cumin
¾ to 1 c. canned black beans,
  drained

¾ to 1 c. canned refried beans
8 8-inch flour tortillas
1 c. guacamole, divided
8-oz. pkg. shredded Mexican
  blend cheese, divided
Garnish: guacamole, sour
  cream, chopped tomatoes

Brown meat in oil in a skillet over medium heat; drain. Stir in enchilada sauce and seasonings; remove from heat. Combine beans in a bowl; stir well and set aside. Place a tortilla in a lightly greased 9" round cake pan; spread with half of bean mixture. Top with another tortilla and half of meat mixture. Add another tortilla and half of guacamole. Add another tortilla and half of cheese. Top with another tortilla. Repeat layers with remaining ingredients except cheese; pan will be full. Cover with aluminum foil. Bake at 350 degrees for 30 minutes. Uncover; sprinkle with remaining cheese. Bake, uncovered, 3 to 5 more minutes, until cheese is melted. Cut into wedges. Serve garnished with favorite toppings. Serves 4.

Katy Thompson
Cartersville, GA

# Melt-in-Your-Mouth Chicken

2 c. cooked chicken, cubed
10¾-oz. can cream of chicken
  soup
2 c. chicken broth
1 c. self-rising flour

1 c. buttermilk
½ c. butter, melted
1 t. salt
½ t. pepper

Arrange chicken in a greased 13"x9" baking pan. Combine soup and broth; mix well and pour over chicken. Mix flour, buttermilk, butter, salt and pepper into batter; spoon over chicken. Bake at 425 degrees for 25 to 30 minutes. Serves 4 to 6.

Karen Norman
Jacksonville, FL

# Chicken Chilaquiles

½ c. oil
10 corn tortillas, cut into
   ½-inch strips
Optional: salt to taste
1 c. shredded mozzarella
   cheese
1 c. shredded Cheddar cheese

2 c. cooked chicken, shredded
28-oz. can mild chile verde
   sauce, divided
Garnish: additional shredded
   mozzarella and Cheddar
   cheeses, chopped fresh
   cilantro

Heat oil in a skillet over medium heat until hot. Cook tortilla strips, a few at a time, just until crispy. Drain tortilla strips on paper towels; sprinkle with salt, if desired. Mix cheeses in a bowl; set aside. Spray a 13"x9" baking pan with non-stick vegetable spray. Layer half of the tortilla strips in pan; top with chicken, one cup sauce and one cup cheese mixture. Press layers gently down into pan. Repeat layering with remaining tortilla strips, sauce and cheese. Bake, uncovered, at 350 degrees for 30 minutes, or until cheese is melted and golden. Garnish with additional cheese and cilantro. Serves 6 to 8.

Sharon Gutierrez
Escondido, CA

"I like to figure out shortcuts to make recipes quick & easy. I combined a few different recipes to make this extremely yummy dinner. Try it…I think you'll agree!"
—Sharon

## make the cut

Put your pizza cutter to work full time. It's perfect for cutting tortillas into strips and slicing cheesy quesadillas into wedges…you're sure to discover other uses!

# Aztec Casserole
Jenny Rubart (Holladay, UT)

2 10-oz. cans enchilada sauce
9 6-inch corn tortillas, halved
1½ to 2 c. sour cream
2 c. shredded Cheddar cheese,
  divided

1 c. salsa
1 c. canned corn
1 lb. boneless, skinless chicken
  breasts, cooked and cubed

Place enchilada sauce in a bowl. Dip 9 tortilla halves in enchilada sauce; arrange in bottom of a lightly greased 13"x9" baking pan and set aside. Combine sour cream, one cup cheese, salsa, corn and chicken in a large bowl; mix well. Spread half of chicken mixture over tortilla halves. Dip remaining tortilla halves in enchilada sauce; repeat layers with remaining tortilla halves and chicken mixture. Sprinkle with remaining cheese; bake, uncovered, at 350 degrees for 25 to 30 minutes. Serves 6 to 8.

## Thai Curry-Coconut Soup

1 c. onion, chopped
1 c. carrots, peeled and diced
1 c. red pepper, diced
1 c. sliced mushrooms
2 t. fresh ginger, peeled and
   grated
½ t. curry powder
2 T. olive oil

32-oz. container coconut
   curry-flavored chicken broth
juice of 2 limes
13½-oz. can coconut milk
1 to 1½ c. cooked chicken or
   shrimp, chopped
¼ c. fresh cilantro, chopped,
   or to taste

"One night I was craving Thai food, so I created this soup by tossing together a few ingredients I had on hand. It turned out to be fabulous!"

–Laurel

Cook vegetables, ginger and curry powder in oil in a Dutch oven over medium heat 3 to 4 minutes. Stir in broth and lime juice. Bring to a boil. Reduce heat; cover and simmer 10 minutes, or until vegetables are soft. Stir in remaining ingredients; heat through. Serves 4.

Laurel Perry
Loganville, GA

# Chicken-Zucchini Casserole

## make-ahead magic

What a time-saver! Most casseroles can be prepared the night before…just cover and refrigerate. Simply add 15 to 20 minutes to the original baking time.

3 c. chicken-flavored stuffing mix
¾ c. butter, melted
3 c. zucchini, diced
2 c. cooked chicken, cubed
1 carrot, peeled and shredded
15-oz. can cream of chicken or mushroom soup
½ c. onion, chopped
½ c. sour cream or softened cream cheese

Mix stuffing and butter in a bowl; reserve ½ cup of mixture for topping. Combine remaining stuffing mixture with remaining ingredients in a large bowl; transfer to a greased 2-quart casserole dish. Top with reserved stuffing mixture. Bake, uncovered, at 350 degrees for 40 to 45 minutes, until hot, bubbly and golden on top. Serves 6 to 8.

Beverly Silver
Telford, PA

# "Chicken Wing" Casserole

4 8-inch flour tortillas
1 to 2 T. olive oil
8-oz. bottle hot pepper sauce or buffalo wing sauce, divided
4 boneless, skinless chicken breasts, cooked and shredded
1 c. light sour cream
2 8-oz. pkgs. Neufchâtel cheese, softened
3 stalks celery, thinly sliced
1-oz. pkg. ranch salad dressing mix
8-oz. pkg. shredded sharp Cheddar cheese, divided

Brush tortillas with oil; place on an ungreased broiler pan. Broil 2 to 3 minutes on each side, until tortillas begin to char and puff. Remove from pan and set aside. Spray a 13"x9" baking pan with non-stick vegetable spray. Spread some sauce lightly in bottom of pan. Line bottom of pan with 2 tortillas; moisten with a little sauce. Reserve a small amount of sauce in a bowl. Mix chicken, sour cream, Neufchâtel cheese, celery, salad dressing mix, remaining sauce and one cup shredded cheese in a large bowl until blended; pat half of mixture into pan. Top with remaining 2 tortillas and moisten with reserved sauce. Top with remaining chicken mixture and shredded cheese. Bake, uncovered, at 350 degrees for 30 to 35 minutes, until bubbly and cheese is melted. Serves 6 to 8.

Graceann Frederico
Bluffton, SC

"Since chicken wings can be expensive, I created this budget-friendly casserole version. When I made this recipe for my church fellowship, it won the grand prize! It was great fun, and I am happy to share it. For variety, omit the tortillas and top with crushed tortilla chips or replace half of the Cheddar cheese with blue cheese."

—Graceann

# Ham + Broccoli Baked Potatoes

2 baking potatoes
½ c. cooked ham, chopped
½ c. broccoli, cooked and chopped
2 slices American cheese
2 t. green onions, chopped

Pierce potatoes with a fork; microwave for 6 to 8 minutes on high until tender. Cut lengthwise and crosswise; squeeze open. Top each potato with ¼ cup each of ham and broccoli. Top each with American cheese. Microwave an additional minute or until cheese is melted; top with green onion. Serves 2.

Linda Behling
Cecil, PA

# Ham Steak & Apples Skillet

3 T. butter
½ c. brown sugar, packed
1 T. Dijon mustard

2 c. apples, cored and sliced
2 1-lb. bone-in ham steaks

Melt butter in a large skillet over medium heat. Add brown sugar and mustard; bring to a simmer. Add apples; cover and simmer 5 minutes. Top apples with ham steaks. Cover and simmer 10 more minutes, or until apples are tender. Remove ham to a platter and cut into serving-size pieces. Top ham with apples and sauce. Serves 6.

Gail Prather
Hastings, NE

> "My grandmother's old black cast-iron skillet brings back wonderful memories of the delicious things she used to make in it. I seek out scrumptious skillet recipes just so I can use Grandma's old skillet...this one has become a real favorite at our house!"
>
> —Gail

# Praline Mustard-Glazed Ham

7 to 8-lb. bone-in, smoked spiral-cut ham half
1 c. maple syrup
¾ c. brown sugar, packed
¾ c. Dijon mustard

⅓ c. apple juice
½ c. raisins
1 c. Granny Smith apple, peeled, cored and thinly sliced

Remove and discard skin and any excess fat from ham. Place in a lightly greased 13"x9" baking pan; insert a meat thermometer into the thickest part of ham. Combine syrup, brown sugar, mustard and apple juice; pour over ham. Set pan on lowest oven rack. Bake at 350 degrees, basting with drippings every 20 minutes, for 2½ hours, or until meat thermometer registers 140 degrees. Let ham stand 10 minutes; remove from pan to a platter, reserving drippings. To make sauce, heat drippings with raisins and apple slices in a small saucepan over low heat 5 minutes. Serve sliced ham with warm sauce. Serves 12.

Sheri Dulaney
Englewood, OH

Ham Steak &
Apples Skillet

# Make-Ahead Ham + Cheese Casserole

"This is one of our favorites for early morning Bible study or mothers' group get-togethers. Remember to prepare this recipe in advance...you'll need to refrigerate it 24 hours before baking."

—Wendy

1 loaf sliced bread, crusts trimmed, divided
10 to 12 slices deli ham, chopped
6-oz. jar sliced mushrooms, drained
10 to 12 slices Cheddar cheese
6 eggs
3 c. milk
½ t. dry mustard
2 c. corn flake cereal, crushed
½ c. butter, melted

Arrange about 8 bread slices in the bottom of a greased 13"x9" baking pan. Top with ham; sprinkle with mushrooms. Arrange cheese slices over mushrooms. Top with remaining bread. Beat eggs, milk and mustard in a bowl; pour over bread. Cover and refrigerate 24 hours. Just before baking, combine cereal and butter in a bowl; sprinkle over top. Bake, uncovered, at 250 degrees for one hour. Serves 10 to 12.

Wendy Deckman
Corona, CA

# Golden Zucchini Crescent Pie

8-oz. tube refrigerated crescent
   rolls
¼ c. butter
2 zucchini, quartered
   lengthwise and sliced
½ c. onion, chopped
2 t. fresh parsley, chopped
½ t. garlic powder
¼ t. dried basil
¼ t. dried oregano
½ t. pepper
2 eggs, beaten
8-oz. pkg. shredded mozzarella
   cheese
¾ c. cooked ham, cubed
1 tomato, thinly sliced
Garnish: fresh parsley sprig

Separate crescent dough into 8 triangles; place in a greased 9" pie plate with points toward the center. Press on bottom and up sides of pie plate to form a crust; press seams together. Bake at 375 degrees for 5 to 8 minutes, until lightly golden. Melt butter in skillet over medium heat. Cook zucchini and onion in melted butter until tender; stir in parsley and seasonings. Spoon into crust. Combine remaining ingredients except tomato and garnish in a bowl; pour over zucchini mixture. Top with tomato slices. Bake, uncovered, at 375 degrees for 20 to 25 minutes, until a knife inserted near center comes out clean. Let stand 5 minutes before cutting. Garnish, if desired. Serves 6.

Diane Cohen
The Woodlands, TX

# Pork Chop-Potato Bake

6 pork chops
salt and pepper to taste
2 T. vegetable oil
10¾-oz. can cream of celery soup
½ c. milk
½ c. sour cream
¼ t. pepper
24-oz. pkg. frozen hashbrowns
   with onions and peppers,
   thawed
1 c. shredded Cheddar cheese
2.8-oz. can French-fried onions

Sprinkle pork chops with salt and pepper; brown in oil and set aside. Combine soup, milk, sour cream, pepper, hashbrowns and cheese; spread into a 13"x9" baking pan. Top with onions and pork chops; bake at 350 degrees for 45 minutes, or until bubbly and golden. Serves 6.

Janet Allen
Hauser, ID

# Grandma Knorberg's Pork Chop Casserole

*This is the ultimate in comfort food!*

6 pork chops, trimmed
salt and pepper to taste
⅛ t. dried sage
10¾-oz. can cream of
   mushroom soup

1 c. carrots, peeled and sliced
½ c. water
½ c. celery, sliced

Arrange pork chops in an ungreased 13"x9" baking pan; sprinkle with salt, pepper and sage. Mix remaining ingredients in a bowl; spoon over chops. Cover and bake at 350 degrees for one hour. Serves 6.

Shirl Parsons
Cape Carteret, NC

# Grandma Jo's Potato Soup

*"My grandma has been making this satisfying soup for as long as I can remember. We really enjoy it on a chilly afternoon."*

—Hope

2 lbs. potatoes, diced
½ lb. carrots, peeled and
   diced
2 stalks celery, diced
1 onion, diced
4 c. water
12-oz. can evaporated milk
¼ c. butter, sliced

seasoned salt with onion &
   garlic to taste
pepper to taste
8-oz. pkg. shredded Cheddar
   cheese
3 slices bacon, crisply cooked
   and crumbled

Combine vegetables and water in a stockpot over medium-high heat. Cook 15 to 20 minutes, until vegetables are fork-tender. Reduce heat to low; stir in evaporated milk, butter and seasonings. Heat through. Ladle into soup bowls; garnish with cheese and bacon. Serves 6.

Hope Davenport
Portland, TX

Grandma Jo's Potato Soup

# South Carolina Gumbo

*Okra imparts a rich flavor to the gumbo and aids in its thickening as it simmers. It's also what gives this gumbo its southern name.*

1 T. olive oil
1 onion, chopped
1 stalk celery, sliced
½ green pepper, chopped
2 c. boneless, skinless chicken breasts, cubed
2 c. okra, chopped
2 14½-oz. cans chicken broth

14½-oz. can diced tomatoes
1 c. water
2 t. Cajun seasoning
1 t. salt
½ t. garlic powder
½ t. pepper
1 c. instant rice, uncooked

Heat oil in a stockpot over medium-high heat. Add onion, celery and green pepper; sauté until tender. Add chicken and remaining ingredients except rice; bring to a boil. Reduce heat and simmer, covered, 15 minutes, or until juices run clear when chicken is pierced. Add rice and simmer 15 more minutes. Serves 6 to 8.

Rachel Reilly
Columbia, SC

## Cajun seasoning

If you don't have any Cajun seasoning on hand, simply stir together ½ teaspoon each of black pepper, white pepper, garlic powder, onion powder, cayenne pepper and paprika.

# Church Supper Tuna Bake

*An old-fashioned favorite that everyone loves.*

¼ c. butter
¾ c. green pepper, diced
3 c. celery, sliced
2 onions, chopped
3 10¾-oz. cans cream of
   mushroom soup
2 c. milk
12-oz. pkg. American cheese,
   cubed

24-oz. pkg. medium egg
   noodles, cooked
1½ c. mayonnaise
4-oz. jar chopped pimentos,
   drained
3 9½-oz. cans tuna, drained
1 c. slivered almonds, toasted

Melt butter in a skillet over medium heat. Add pepper, celery and onions; sauté 10 minutes, or until tender. Combine soup and milk in a large stockpot; add vegetable mixture and cook over medium heat until heated through. Stir in cheese until melted. Mix cooked noodles and 2 cups soup mixture in a large bowl; toss to coat. Spread in 2 lightly greased 13"x9" baking pans. Stir mayonnaise, pimentos and tuna into remaining soup mixture. Pour over noodles and mix gently; sprinkle with almonds. Bake, uncovered, at 375 degrees for 35 to 40 minutes. Serves 25.

## make-ahead magic

Save time by cooking a casserole ahead…it's easy! Line the casserole dish with aluminum foil, leaving a 2-inch overhang around edges. Add casserole ingredients, bake as directed, cool and freeze, uncovered. When completely frozen, lift the casserole out using aluminum foil overhang. Cover and freeze. To thaw, simply place in the casserole dish it was originally baked in.

# New England Fish Chowder

1 T. vegetable oil
½ c. onion, chopped
2½ c. potato, peeled and diced
1½ c. boiling water
salt and pepper to taste

1 lb. frozen cod or haddock fillets, thawed and cut into large chunks
2 c. milk
1 T. butter
Garnish: fresh parsley sprigs

Heat oil in a large saucepan over medium heat. Add onion; cook until tender. Add potato, water, salt and pepper. Reduce heat; cover and simmer 15 to 20 minutes, until potatoes are tender. Add fish; simmer about 5 minutes, until fish flakes easily with a fork. Add milk and butter just before serving; heat through. Garnish servings with parsley sprigs. Serves 6.

# Creamy Potato-Clam Bisque

¼ c. butter
1 onion, chopped
1 c. celery, chopped
4 slices bacon, crisply cooked
 and crumbled
⅛ c. fresh parsley, chopped
½ t. salt

¼ t. pepper
4 potatoes, diced
1 qt. chicken broth
3 T. cornstarch
¼ c. water
1 qt. half-and-half
3 6-oz. cans clams

*"Our family loves this chowder-type soup… when I serve it to company, I'm always asked for the recipe."*

*—Corinne*

Melt butter in a Dutch oven over medium heat. Sauté onion, celery and bacon in melted butter 10 minutes; add parsley, salt, pepper, potatoes and broth. Cover and cook over medium heat 30 minutes. Whisk together cornstarch and water in a medium bowl; add half-and-half and clams with juice. Pour into broth; simmer, without boiling, until heated through. Serves 6 to 8.

Corinne Gross
Tigard, OR

# Curried Harvest Bisque

1 lb. butternut squash,
 peeled and cut into 1-inch
 cubes
5 c. chicken broth
¼ c. butter
¼ c. all-purpose flour

3 T. curry powder
¾ c. half-and-half
3 T. lime juice
½ t. salt
¼ t. white pepper

Combine squash and broth in a heavy 4-quart sockpot. Cook over medium heat about 15 minutes, or until squash is tender. Using a slotted spoon, transfer squash to a blender or food processor; process until smooth. Stir broth into puréed squash; set aside. Melt butter in stockpot; stir in flour and curry powder. Cook over medium heat, stirring until smooth. Add squash mixture; increase heat to medium-high and stir until soup thickens slightly. Reduce heat to low. Add half-and-half and remaining ingredients; and heat thoroughly (do not boil). Serves 6.

Kathy Grashoff
Fort Wayne, IN

# One-Dish Reuben Dinner

16-oz. can sauerkraut, undrained
1 lb. deli corned beef, chopped
2 c. shredded Swiss cheese
½ c. mayonnaise
¼ c. Thousand Island salad dressing

2 c. tomatoes, sliced
¼ to ½ c. pumpernickel or rye soft bread crumbs
2 T. butter, melted

Place sauerkraut in a lightly greased 1½-quart casserole dish. Top with corned beef and cheese. Combine mayonnaise and salad dressing in a small bowl; spread over cheese. Arrange tomatoes on top. Toss together bread crumbs and melted butter in a bowl; sprinkle over top of casserole. Bake, uncovered, at 350 degrees for 25 to 30 minutes. Let stand 5 minutes before serving. Serves 4 to 6.

Suzanne Ruminski
Johnson City, NY

# Baked Potato Soup

3 lbs. redskin potatoes,
  cubed
¼ c. butter
¼ c. all-purpose flour
2 qts. half-and-half
16-oz. pkg. pasteurized process
  cheese spread, cubed

1 t. hot pepper sauce
white pepper and garlic
  powder to taste
Toppings: crumbled cooked
  bacon, shredded Cheddar
  cheese, snipped fresh chives

## toss-ins for a twist

Cubed cooked ham, chopped
cooked broccoli and a dollop
of sour cream would make
another tasty topping trio
to mimic a traditional baked
potato.

Cover potatoes with water in a large saucepan; bring to a boil. Boil
10 minutes, or until tender; drain and set aside. Melt butter in a large
Dutch oven; add flour, stirring until smooth. Gradually add half-and-half,
stirring constantly over low heat, until smooth and mixture begins to
thicken. Add cheese; stir well. Add potatoes, sauce and seasonings. Cover
and simmer over low heat 30 minutes. Add desired toppings. Serves 8.

Linda Stone
Cookeville, TN

# Fettuccine Alfredo

¼ c. butter
3 T. all-purpose flour
2 c. milk
⅛ t. cayenne pepper
¼ t. salt

⅛ t. white pepper
1½ c. grated Parmesan cheese,
  divided
12-oz. pkg fettuccine, cooked

In a 2-quart glass bowl, microwave butter, uncovered, on high one
minute. Stir in flour and blend well. Stir in milk, cayenne pepper, salt and
white pepper. Microwave, uncovered, on high 4 to 5 minutes, until thickened, stirring twice. Stir in one cup Parmesan cheese until melted. Toss
with pasta; sprinkle with remaining cheese. Serves 4.

# Beefy Tortilla Casserole

*Super-easy dish for the microwave!*

## toss-ins for a twist

Green or red peppers also make a nice addition to this dish. If you have extras on hand, just add ½ cup for additional flavor.

1 lb. ground beef
4-oz. can diced green chiles, drained
½ onion, chopped
salt to taste
1 c. picante sauce
10¾-oz. can cream of mushroom soup
8-oz. container sour cream
6 corn tortillas, cut into 1-inch wide strips and divided
1 c. shredded Cheddar cheese, divided
½ c. shredded mozzarella cheese
Optional: paprika, dried parsley

Crumble beef into an ungreased one-quart casserole dish. Microwave, uncovered, on high 3 minutes; drain. Add green chiles, onion and salt; microwave 3 minutes longer. Stir in picante sauce. Mix soup and sour cream in a small bowl; set aside. Arrange one-third of the tortilla strips in a greased 2-quart casserole dish; top with half of the beef mixture and one-third of the Cheddar cheese. Repeat layers, ending with tortilla strips. Pour soup mixture over top. Microwave, uncovered, on high 5 minutes. Top with remaining cheeses; microwave, uncovered, until melted. Just before serving, sprinkle lightly with paprika and parsley, if desired. Serves 6.

# Easy Goulash

1 lb. ground beef
¼ c. onion, chopped
14½-oz. can stewed tomatoes
¾ c. water
salt and pepper to taste
2 c. elbow macaroni, uncooked
15¼-oz. can corn, drained
15-oz. can kidney beans, drained and rinsed
16-oz. pkg. pasteurized process cheese spread, cubed

Brown beef and onion in a large stockpot; drain. Add tomatoes and water; sprinkle with salt and pepper to taste. Add macaroni and simmer 8 to 10 minutes, or until macaroni is tender, adding more water if necessary. Add corn, beans and cheese; heat and stir until cheese is melted. Serves 4 to 6.

Kimberly Basore
Garland, TX

## Wild Rice Hot Dish
June Sabatinos (Billings, MT)

2 lbs. ground beef
½ c. butter
1 lb. sliced mushrooms
1 c. onion, chopped
½ c. celery, chopped
2 c. sour cream

¼ c. soy sauce
2 t. salt
¼ t. pepper
2 c. long-grain and wild rice, cooked
½ c. slivered almonds

Brown beef in a skillet over medium heat. Remove beef from skillet; drain. Melt butter in skillet over medium heat; sauté mushrooms, onion and celery in melted butter 5 to 10 minutes, until tender. Combine sour cream, soy sauce, salt and pepper in a large bowl. Stir in beef, mushroom mixture, cooked rice and almonds. Place mixture in a greased 3-quart casserole dish. Bake, uncovered, at 350 degrees for one hour, or until heated through. Stir occasionally, adding a little water, if needed. Serves 12 to 16.

# Paula's Baked Ziti

*"This is our most-requested dish at every potluck... it's super simple to make, too."*

*—Theresa*

1 lb. ground beef, browned and drained
4 c. ziti pasta, cooked
28-oz. jar spaghetti sauce
1 c. grated Parmesan-Romano cheese, divided
8-oz. pkg. shredded mozzarella cheese

Combine beef, pasta, sauce and ¾ cup grated cheese in a large bowl; mix well. Spread in a lightly greased 13"x9" baking pan; sprinkle with mozzarella cheese. Bake, uncovered, at 375 degrees for 20 minutes, or until hot and bubbly. Garnish with remaining grated cheese. Serves 6.

Theresa Reynolds
Groton, CT

# Nana's Hamburger Pie

1 onion, chopped
2 to 3 t. oil
1 lb. ground beef
¾ t. salt
⅛ t. pepper

2 c. fresh green beans, trimmed
10¾-oz. can tomato soup
Optional: shredded Cheddar cheese

Cook onion in oil in a skillet over medium heat until tender. Add beef, salt and pepper; brown lightly and drain. Add green beans and soup; mix well. Spoon into a greased 1½-quart casserole dish. Drop Potato Fluff Topping in mounds over beef mixture. Sprinkle cheese over topping, if desired. Bake, uncovered, at 350 degrees for 25 to 30 minutes. Serves 6.

# Potato Fluff Topping:

5 potatoes, peeled, chopped and cooked
½ c. warm milk

1 egg, beaten
salt and pepper to taste

While still warm, mash potatoes with remaining ingredients.

## in a hurry?

Instead of peeling, chopping and cooking the potatoes, replace the Potato Fluff Topping with refrigerated mashed potatoes prepared as directed on package.

# Beefy Cheddar Bake

*"This was my grandmother's casserole recipe. Mom made it for her family, and now I make it for mine. It's delicious and a great dish for sharing. Everyone I've ever made this for loves it and asks to have it again. Go ahead and reheat it the next day...it's just as good!"*

*–Kimberly*

1 lb. ground beef
1 onion, chopped
1 green pepper, chopped
14½-oz. can diced tomatoes, drained
8-oz. pkg. shredded sharp Cheddar cheese
2 c. rotini pasta, cooked
10¾-oz. can cream of mushroom soup
6-oz. can French-fried onions

Brown beef with onion and pepper in a skillet over medium-high heat; drain. Combine all ingredients except French-fried onions in a large bowl; mix well. Transfer mixture to a lightly greased 13"x9" baking pan; cover with aluminum foil. Bake at 350 degrees for 30 minutes. Remove foil; sprinkle with French-fried onions. Bake, uncovered, 5 to 10 more minutes. Serves 8 to 12.

Kimberly Keafer
Johnsbury, VT

# Easy Cheesy Manicotti

12-oz. pkg. manicotti, uncooked
1½ t. salt, divided
1 T. olive oil
8-oz. pkg. cream cheese, softened
2 c. cottage cheese
12-oz. pkg. shredded Monterey Jack cheese
1 egg, beaten
1 T. fresh parsley, chopped
1 clove garlic, minced
12-oz. pkg. shredded mozzarella cheese, divided
24-oz. jar spaghetti sauce

Cook manicotti according to package directions, using one teaspoon salt and one tablespoon oil; drain and set aside. Combine cheeses, egg, parsley, garlic, remaining ½ teaspoon salt and two-thirds of the mozzarella cheese in a large bowl; set aside. Spread a thin layer of spaghetti sauce on the bottom of an ungreased 13"x9" baking pan. Spoon cheese filling into each manicotti noodle, filling three-fourths full; arrange on top of sauce. Pour remaining sauce over manicotti; bake, uncovered, at 350 degrees for 30 to 45 minutes. Top with remaining mozzarella 10 minutes before done. Cool 10 minutes before serving. Serves 6.

Robin Argyle
Kalkaska, MI

# Mary's Macaroni + Cheese

16-oz. pkg. elbow macaroni, cooked

16-oz. container sharp pasteurized process cheese spread

2 c. shredded Colby Jack cheese

12-oz. can evaporated milk

½ c. butter, diced

2 eggs, beaten

1 c. shredded Cheddar cheese

1 c. panko bread crumbs or plain dry bread crumbs

Mix together all ingredients except Cheddar cheese and bread crumbs in a large bowl. Pour into a greased 13"x9" baking pan. Top with Cheddar cheese and bread crumbs. Bake, uncovered, at 350 degrees for 30 minutes, or until bubbly and golden. Serves 10.

Creamy Bacon &
Herb Succotash,
page 160

# sensational side dishes

Make any meal complete with one of these appetizing side dishes. They're so simple and full of goodness! Creamy and comforting, Corny Macaroni Casserole is a hands-down favorite. Tomato-Mozzarella Salad and Fried Okra Salad provide a burst of fresh flavor.

# Yellow Rice + Corn Bake

*"My friend gave me this recipe at a workplace potluck. Wherever I take it, it's always the talk of the meal!"*

—Beverly

5-oz. pkg. saffron yellow rice mix

2 11-oz. cans sweet corn & diced peppers

10¾-oz. can cream of celery soup

1 c. shredded Cheddar cheese

½ c. butter, softened

Prepare rice according to package directions. Stir in remaining ingredients. Transfer to a greased 2-quart casserole dish. Bake, uncovered, at 350 degrees for 30 to 35 minutes, until hot and bubbly. Serves 4 to 6.

Beverly Sensebe
Vancleave, MS

# Abuela's Garlic Grits

4½ c. water
1 t. salt
1 c. quick-cooking grits,
   uncooked
½ c. butter, cubed
¾ lb. pasteurized process
   cheese spread, cubed

2 eggs
⅔ c. milk
¼ t. garlic powder
1 c. wheat & barley cereal
hot pepper sauce to taste

Bring water and salt to a boil in a saucepan over high heat. Slowly stir in grits; cook 3 to 5 minutes, stirring constantly. Remove from heat. Add butter and cheese, stirring until melted. Beat eggs, milk and garlic powder in a bowl; stir into hot mixture. Pour into an ungreased 13"x9" glass baking pan. Sprinkle with cereal and hot sauce. Bake, uncovered, at 350 degrees for one hour. Let stand 15 minutes before serving. Serves 10 to 12.

Kelly Petty
Aiken, SC

"My grandmother's most-requested recipe. Her name was Frances, but my daughter lovingly called her Abuela (Spanish for grandmother) because she was a Spanish professor."

—Kelly

Corny Macaroni Casserole

## Corny Macaroni Casserole

*Two favorite side dishes combine to make one outstanding casserole!*

15¼-oz. can corn
14¾-oz. can creamed corn
1 c. elbow macaroni, uncooked
1 c. pasteurized process
    cheese spread, cubed
½ c. butter, melted

*"I like to double this recipe for a yummy potluck dish."*
—Deb

    Mix together all ingredients in a large bowl. Transfer to a greased 2-quart casserole dish. Cover and bake at 350 degrees for 40 minutes. Uncover and bake 20 more minutes. Serves 4 to 6.

Deb Blean
Morrison, IL

## Artichoke-Tortellini Salad

*A make-ahead salad that's perfect for toting to a picnic in the park, girlfriends' lunch or backyard cookout.*

7-oz. pkg. refrigerated
    cheese tortellini
1 c. broccoli florets
6-oz. jar marinated artichoke
    hearts, drained
½ c. fresh parsley, finely
    chopped
1 T. pimento, chopped
2 green onions, chopped
1½ t. fresh basil, chopped, or
    ¼ t. dried basil
½ t. garlic powder
½ c. Italian salad dressing
5 to 6 cherry tomatoes, halved
Garnish: sliced black olives,
    grated Parmesan cheese

    Cook tortellini according to package directions. Drain and rinse with cool water. Combine all ingredients except tomatoes and garnish in a large bowl. Cover and refrigerate 4 to 6 hours to blend flavors. When ready to serve, add tomatoes and toss lightly. Garnish with olives and cheese. Serves 6.

Kay Barg
Sandy, UT

# Colorful Couscous Salad

*Look for flavored couscous in the pasta aisle...so tasty and easy!*

## toss-ins for a twist

Serve up individual portions of this colorful dish in edible bowls. Hollow out fresh green or red peppers and fill 'em for a quick and tasty lunch.

10-oz. pkg. couscous, uncooked
¾ c. olive oil
¼ c. lemon juice
⅛ c. white wine vinegar
2 T. sugar
1 T. garlic, minced
3 drops hot pepper sauce
½ t. salt
½ t. pepper
½ t. lemon pepper
½ t. seasoned salt
¼ t. turmeric
⅛ t. cinnamon
⅛ t. ground ginger
1 green pepper, diced
1 bunch green onions, diced
4 carrots, shredded
15¼-oz. can corn, drained
15½-oz. can black beans, drained and rinsed

Prepare couscous according to package directions; drain and set aside. Whisk together olive oil, lemon juice, vinegar, sugar, garlic, hot sauce and seasonings in a large serving bowl; stir in vegetables and beans. Add couscous, mixing well. Cover and refrigerate until serving time. Serves 6 to 8.

Donna Cash
Dexter, MI

# Wheat Berry + Wild Rice Salad

1 c. wheat berries, uncooked
1 c. wild rice, uncooked
1 red or green pepper, diced
1 red onion, chopped
½ c. walnuts, toasted and
   coarsely chopped
¼ c. fresh oregano, chopped
4 to 5 leaves fresh basil,
   chopped
3 sprigs fresh parsley, chopped
vinaigrette salad dressing
   to taste

Cover wheat berries with water in a saucepan; cover with lid and soak 8 hours to overnight. Drain wheat berries well; add fresh cold water to cover. Cook over medium heat one hour, or until tender; drain well. Meanwhile, in a separate saucepan, cover rice with cold water. Cook over medium heat 30 minutes, or until tender; drain well. Combine wheat berries and rice in a serving bowl. Stir in remaining ingredients, adding salad dressing to taste. For the best flavor, serve at room temperature; may also be served chilled. Serves 6 to 9.

Linda Karner
Pisgah Forest, NC

"This is a recipe I made up myself, and my family loves it! You can add any fresh herbs that you like. Be sure to allow enough time for the wheat berries to soak."

–Linda

## wheat berry wisdom

Wheat berries aren't actually berries at all…they're whole kernels of wheat, comparable to brown rice or hulled barley. Look for them at farm stands or in the pasta and grain aisle of the grocery store.

## Tomato Salad with Grilled Bread

"I found this unusual recipe and then tweaked it to make it my own. It's great for backyard barbecues. I guarantee you'll like it, too!"

—Bev

3 lbs. tomatoes, cut into chunks
1 cucumber, peeled and sliced
4-oz. container crumbled feta cheese
¼ c. balsamic vinegar
¼ t. salt
¼ t. pepper
8 thick slices crusty Italian bread, cubed

2 c. watermelon, cut into ½-inch cubes
1 red onion, very thinly sliced and separated into rings
3.8-oz. can sliced black olives, drained
¼ c. plus ½ t. olive oil
½ c. fresh basil, torn

Combine tomatoes, cucumber, cheese, vinegar, salt and pepper in a large serving bowl. Toss to mix; cover and chill one hour. Place bread cubes on an ungreased baking sheet. Bake at 350 degrees for 5 minutes, or until lightly golden. At serving time, add bread cubes and remaining ingredients to tomato mixture. Toss very lightly and serve. Serves 6.

Bev Fisher
Mesa, AZ

# Italian Salad Bowl

*One day I was trying to come up with a new salad to go with our spaghetti for dinner. This salad was a hit with my family…it seems everyone has a favorite ingredient in it! Feel free to add any fresh herbs from your garden.*

2 c. cherry tomatoes
½ lb. bite-size mozzarella cheese balls, drained
1 cucumber, peeled, halved lengthwise and sliced into half-moons
2 6-oz. jars marinated artichoke hearts, drained

6-oz. can black olives, drained
6-oz. pkg. turkey pepperoni slices
1 c. fat-free Italian salad dressing
Optional: chopped fresh oregano, parsley and/or other herbs

Combine all ingredients in a large bowl; toss gently. Cover and refrigerate about 2 hours before serving to allow flavors to blend. Serves 6.

Teri Lindquist
Gurnee, IL

## a colorful touch

Keep a bunch of fresh green parsley in the fridge, ready to add a little color and a taste of the garden to meals anytime. Simply place the bunch, stems down, in a glass of water and cover the top loosely with a plastic sandwich bag. It'll stay fresh and flavorful for more than a week.

# Creamy Bacon + Herb Succotash

"You'll love this deluxe version of an old harvest-time favorite...I do!"

—Vickie

¼ lb. bacon, chopped
1 onion, diced
10-oz. pkg. frozen lima beans
½ c. water
salt and pepper to taste

10-oz. pkg. frozen corn
½ c. whipping cream
1½ t. fresh thyme, minced
Garnish: 2 t. fresh chives, snipped

Cook bacon until crisp in a Dutch oven over medium-high heat. Remove bacon, reserving 2 tablespoons drippings in Dutch oven. Add onion; sauté about 5 minutes, or until tender. Add beans, water, salt and pepper; bring to a boil. Reduce heat; cover and simmer 5 minutes. Stir in corn, whipping cream and thyme; return to a simmer. Cook until vegetables are tender, about 5 minutes. Toss with bacon and chives before serving. Serves 6.

Vickie
Gooseberry Patch

# Strawberry-Melon Salad

1 cantaloupe, peeled, seeded and cubed

1 honeydew or Crenshaw melon, peeled, seeded and cubed

2 c. strawberries, hulled and quartered

*"I love to make this dish during strawberry season. It's light yet filling."*
*—Sandra*

Combine melon cubes in a large bowl. Drizzle with Banana-Yogurt Dressing; toss to mix. Top with strawberries and serve immediately. Serves 4.

# Banana-Yogurt Dressing:

½ c. plain low-fat yogurt

½ c. orange juice

1 banana, sliced

Place all ingredients in a blender or food processor. Cover and blend until puréed.

Sandra Bins
Georgetown, TX

# Penne + Goat Cheese Salad

12-oz. pkg. penne pasta, uncooked

1 T. garlic, minced

¼ c. mayonnaise

6-oz. pkg. goat cheese, diced

½ c. sun-dried tomatoes packed in oil, drained and oil reserved

2 c. baby spinach

*"One of my husband's favorite pasta salads... it's just a little different from most. Try arugula for a slightly spicy taste or feta cheese if you prefer it to goat cheese."*
*—Claudia*

Cook pasta according to package directions; drain and rinse with cold water. Combine pasta with garlic, mayonnaise and goat cheese in a large bowl. Finely chop tomatoes and add along with spinach; mix gently. Stir in reserved oil from tomatoes, one tablespoon at a time, until ingredients are coated. Serve at room temperature or cover and chill. Serves 8.

Claudia Olsen
Chester, NJ

# Spinach, Strawberry + Walnut Salad

1½ lbs. spinach, torn
3 c. strawberries, hulled and sliced

1 sweet onion, thinly sliced
1 c. chopped walnuts

Arrange spinach, strawberries, onion and nuts in a salad bowl. Cover and refrigerate. Drizzle desired amount of Poppy Seed Dressing over salad just before serving. Toss and serve immediately. Serves 6.

## Poppy Seed Dressing:

¾ c. sugar
1 t. dry mustard
1 t. salt
⅓ c. cider vinegar

2 t. green onion, chopped
¾ to 1 c. olive oil
1½ T. poppy seed

Place sugar, mustard, salt and vinegar in a blender; cover and blend until smooth. Add onion and blend until smooth. With blender running, add oil slowly. Cover and blend until thick. Stir in poppy seed.

Cheryl Donnelly
Arvada, CO

## serving secret
Serve up salad dressings in old-fashioned pint milk bottles...charming!

# Tomato-Mozzarella Salad

Joanna Nicoline-Haughey (Berwyn, PA)

*I remember Mom serving this simple salad in the summertime, made with fresh ingredients from Dad's wonderful garden full of sun-ripe tomatoes, cucumbers, green peppers and herbs. What great memories!*

4 tomatoes, cubed
1 cucumber, sliced
1 c. mozzarella cheese, cubed

1 T. fresh basil, chopped
¼ c. extra-virgin olive oil
salt and pepper to taste

Mix tomatoes, cucumber, cheese and basil in a serving bowl. Drizzle with oil and toss to mix; sprinkle with salt and pepper. Serves 4.

# Mother's Cucumber Salad

"This is my mother's recipe...it always reminds me of summer and picnics. Cool, crisp, not to mention delicious, it tastes even better the longer it marinates in the refrigerator."

—Amy

3 to 4 cucumbers, peeled and thinly sliced
3 T. salt
2 T. sugar
½ t. onion powder
¼ t. celery seed
¼ t. pepper
¼ c. cider vinegar
Optional: ½ c. sliced red onion

Place cucumbers in a large bowl; add salt and enough water to cover. Cover and shake to combine. Refrigerate several hours to overnight. Drain cucumbers, but do not rinse; return to bowl. Stir together sugar, onion powder, celery seed, pepper and vinegar in a small bowl; mix well. Pour vinegar mixture over cucumbers. Add onion, if desired. Cover and shake gently to mix. Serves 6.

Amy Gerhart
Farmington, MI

# Fully Loaded Mashed Potatoes

6 potatoes, peeled and
    quartered
¼ c. butter, softened
½ c. sour cream
½ t. salt

⅛ t. pepper
4 slices bacon, crisply cooked
    and crumbled
½ c. shredded Cheddar cheese
4 green onions, thinly sliced

Place potatoes in a saucepan and cover with water. Bring to a boil over medium-high heat; reduce heat and cover. Simmer 15 to 20 minutes, until fork-tender; drain. Mash potatoes with a potato masher or beat with an electric mixer on low speed. Add butter, sour cream, salt and pepper; mash or beat until potatoes are fluffy. Stir in remaining ingredients. Serves 6.

Norma Burton
Kuna, ID

"I was going to prepare individual baked potatoes for dinner but needed to hurry, so I mashed all the ingredients together instead... everyone loved it!"

—Norma

# Crispy Potato Fingers

3 c. corn flake cereal
3 T. grated Parmesan cheese
1 T. paprika
¼ t. garlic salt

¼ c. butter, melted
2 potatoes, peeled and cut into
    strips

Place cereal, cheese and seasonings in a blender or food processor. Cover and blend until crushed and well mixed. Pour cereal mixture into a pie plate or shallow dish; place melted butter in a separate shallow dish. Dip potato strips in butter and then in cereal mixture, coating well. Arrange potato strips on a greased baking sheet. Bake at 375 degrees for 25 minutes, or until tender and golden. Serves 4.

Lisa Johnson
Hallsville, TX

"My mama always made these 'tater fingers' for my kids when they came for a visit. The kids are both grown now, but they still love it when Granny makes these yummy potatoes!"

—Lisa

## Summer Stuffed Tomatoes

4 tomatoes
salt to taste
2½ c. corn, divided
3 eggs, beaten

¼ c. grated Parmesan cheese
1 T. fresh basil, finely chopped
salt and pepper to taste
4 slices provolone cheese

Cut ½-inch tops off tomatoes; scoop out insides. Lightly sprinkle insides of tomatoes with salt; turn tomatoes upside-down in a dish. Purée 1½ cups corn, eggs and Parmesan cheese in a food processor. Stir in remaining one cup corn, basil, salt and pepper; mix well. Spoon into tomatoes; arrange in a lightly greased 9"x9" baking pan. Bake, uncovered, at 400 degrees for 40 minutes; place a cheese slice over each tomato and bake 5 more minutes. Remove from oven and let stand a few minutes before serving. Serves 4.

*"This is actually my sister's recipe, but it's so good that I had to share it! One of my favorite summer side dishes, these tomatoes are excellent with sweet corn fresh from your garden."*

–Jennifer

Jennifer Oglesby
Brownsville, IN

# Grandma Lucy's Corn Fritters

*Showcase the bounty of summer corn with a batch of these delicately fried fritters. When sweet corn is not at its peak, substitute 3 cups of canned or frozen corn kernels.*

4 ears sweet corn, cooked
2 eggs, beaten
¼ c. milk
½ c. all-purpose flour
1 t. baking powder
1 t. sugar

½ t. salt
1 t. bacon drippings or
   vegetable oil
Optional: butter, maple syrup

*"These fritters remind me of my childhood and the golden days of summer when my grandmother made them."*

*—Carole*

Cut kernels from corn and place in a medium mixing bowl; stir in eggs and milk. Combine flour, baking powder, sugar and salt in a small bowl; stir into corn mixture, mixing gently. Heat bacon drippings or vegetable oil in a skillet over medium-high heat. Drop batter by ¼ cupfuls into skillet and cook until lightly browned, flipping to brown the other side. Serve with butter and maple syrup, if desired. Makes one dozen.

Carole Griffin
Mount Vernon, OH

# Copper-Penny Carrots

*A tasty recipe that goes way back! It can be refrigerated for two weeks, so it's a convenient make-ahead to keep on hand.*

2 lbs. carrots, peeled and sliced
1 green pepper, thinly sliced
1 onion, chopped
10¾-oz. can tomato soup
¾ to 1 c. sugar
¾ c. cider vinegar
½ c. vegetable oil
1 t. Worcestershire sauce
1 t. mustard
salt and pepper to taste

Cook carrots in salted water in a saucepan over medium heat until almost tender; drain and rinse. Transfer carrots to a serving bowl; set aside. Combine remaining ingredients in a separate saucepan. Bring to a boil over medium heat, stirring until thoroughly blended. Pour soup mixture over carrots. Cover and refrigerate until flavors are blended, at least 24 hours. Serves 10 to 12.

Evelyn Love
Standish, ME

# Feta Beans

*This is such a great side dish. You can use canned or frozen green beans, but it is especially good with green beans right from the garden!*

16-oz. pkg. frozen green beans
¼ c. butter
16-oz. pkg. sliced mushrooms
1 onion, finely diced
2 cloves garlic, minced
1 t. salt
½ t. pepper
4-oz. container crumbled feta cheese

Prepare green beans according to package directions; drain. Melt butter in a large skillet over medium heat. Add mushrooms, onion, garlic, salt and pepper. Cook 5 to 7 minutes, until heated through. Stir in cheese. Serve immediately. Serves 8 to 10.

Cyndy DeStefano
Mercer, PA

# Baked Corn
Melissa Garland (Annville, PA)

2 eggs, beaten
1 c. sour cream
15-oz. can creamed corn

15¼-oz. can corn
7-oz. pkg. corn muffin mix
½ c. butter, softened

Combine eggs and sour cream in a large bowl; add creamed corn and corn, mixing well. Stir in muffin mix; add butter. Pour into a lightly greased 8"x8" baking pan. Bake, uncovered, at 350 degrees for 35 to 45 minutes. Serves 12.

# Fried Okra Salad

*The okra soaks up all the yummy sweet vinaigrette in the salad…a nice contrast to the crunchy bacon.*

2-lb. pkg. frozen breaded okra
10 slices bacon, crisply cooked
   and crumbled
6 roma tomatoes, chopped

1 bunch green onions, chopped
½ c. olive oil
¼ c. sugar
2 T. vinegar

Fry okra according to package directions; drain. Combine okra, bacon, tomatoes and green onions in a serving bowl; set aside. Mix together remaining ingredients in a small bowl; pour dressing over okra mixture. Best served at room temperature. Serve immediately. Serves 8.

Lisa Martin
Tulsa, OK

*"I took this dish to a ladies' function at my church, and by the time it was over, everyone had copied the recipe!"*

*—Lisa*

## to market

Visit the farmers' market for the best homegrown veggies…toss a market basket in the car, and let the kids pick out fresh flavors for Sunday dinner!

Fresh Strawberry
Shortcake, page 200

# prize-winning desserts

End the meal right with one of these special treats. Rich & creamy Mocha-Pecan Mud Pie tastes so good topped with frozen whipped topping and crushed cookies. No one can resist Granny's Chocolate Fudge Cookies or Lemon-Coconut Bars. From cakes and pies to cookies and other sweet treats…leave plenty of room for dessert!

# Hasty Peach Cobbler

*This recipe is a lifesaver when you have last-minute dinner guests. Mix it up quick, pop it in the oven and by the time you've finished dinner, a scrumptious warm dessert is ready.*

## toss-ins for a twist

Substitute apple pie filling for the peach pie filling for a scrumptious fall treat.

½ c. all-purpose flour
½ c. sugar
1 t. baking powder
½ c. milk

2 T. butter, diced
21-oz. can peach pie filling
Garnish: vanilla ice cream

Mix together flour, sugar and baking powder in a bowl. Add milk and stir to mix well. Dot an ungreased 9"x9" baking pan with butter; pour batter into pan. Spoon peaches over batter. Bake at 375 degrees for 30 minutes, or until golden. Serve warm, topped with a scoop of ice cream. Serves 6.

Cynthia Green
Worthington, IN

# Pineapple-Cherry Cake

*Serve with either whipped topping or ice cream.*

20-oz. can crushed pineapple
18¼-oz. pkg. yellow cake mix, divided
15½-oz. can pitted cherries, drained

1 c. chopped walnuts or pecans
1 c. butter, melted
Optional: frozen whipped topping, thawed

Evenly spoon pineapple into an ungreased 13"x9" baking pan. Sprinkle half the cake mix on top; spread cherries over cake mix. Sprinkle remaining cake mix over cherries; top with nuts. Drizzle with butter; bake at 350 degrees for 45 to 50 minutes. Garnish with whipped topping, if desired. Serves 15.

David Flory
Columbus, OH

Pineapple-Cherry
Cake

Grandma's
Pecan Balls

# Just Peachy Blueberry Crisp

3 c. peaches, peeled, pitted and
   sliced
½ c. blueberries
2 t. cinnamon-sugar
1 c. all-purpose flour

1 c. brown sugar, packed
½ c. butter
¾ c. long-cooking oats,
   uncooked

Arrange peaches and blueberries in a buttered 8"x8" baking pan. Sprinkle with cinnamon-sugar; toss gently to coat. Combine flour and brown sugar in a bowl; cut in butter and oats. Sprinkle evenly over peach mixture. Bake at 350 degrees for 40 to 45 minutes. Serves 6 to 8.

Kristin Pittis
Dennison, OH

*"I came up with this recipe when I had a basket of fresh peaches...it's so good!"*
—Kristin

# Grandma's Pecan Balls

*Include this old-fashioned classic on your holiday sideboard.*

1 c. butter, softened
⅓ c. sugar
2 t. vanilla extract

2 c. all-purpose flour
2 c. pecans, chopped
Garnish: powdered sugar

Blend butter and sugar in a medium bowl; stir in vanilla and flour. Stir in pecans. Roll dough into walnut-size balls; arrange on an ungreased baking sheet. Bake at 325 degrees for 45 minutes. While still warm, sprinkle cookies with powdered sugar; sprinkle again before serving. Makes about 2 dozen.

Beckie Butcher
Elgin, IL

*"My Grandma Caroline always made these for Christmas...they were a treat I looked forward to. They remind me of a truly old-fashioned family holiday."*
—Beckie

# Lemon-Macadamia Cookies

¾ c. butter, softened
1 c. sugar
1 c. brown sugar, packed
2 eggs
3.4-oz. pkg. instant lemon
   pudding mix
2¼ c. all-purpose flour

1 t. baking soda
¼ t. salt
2 t. lemon zest
1 t. lemon extract
1 c. macadamia nuts, coarsely
   chopped
½ c. toffee baking bits

Beat butter and sugars in a large bowl with an electric mixer at medium speed until light and fluffy. Add eggs, one at a time, beating until blended after each addition. Combine dry pudding mix, flour, baking soda, salt and zest in a separate bowl. Slowly add pudding mixture to butter mixture. Add extract; beat until combined. Stir in nuts and toffee bits. Drop by rounded tablespoonfuls onto ungreased baking sheets 2 inches apart. Bake at 350 degrees for 10 to 13 minutes, until lightly golden around edges. Cool cookies on baking sheets 2 minutes. Remove to wire racks to cool completely. Store in an airtight container. Makes 4 dozen.

Brenda Melancon
Gonzales, LA

## so versatile

A one-gallon glass apothecary jar makes a great cookie jar. Before using, thoroughly wash jar with hot soapy water and dry completely. Personalize it by using a glass paint pen to add a message such as "Family Favorite Cookies." Add hearts or swirls just for fun.

# German Chocolate Cookies

18¼-oz. pkg. German
  chocolate cake mix
¼ c. vegetable oil

3 eggs, beaten
14½-oz. can coconut-pecan
  frosting

Combine dry cake mix, oil and eggs in a large bowl. Beat with an electric mixer at medium-high speed until thoroughly blended. Roll into one-inch balls; place one inch apart on baking sheets sprayed with non-stick vegetable spray. Bake at 350 degrees for about 8 minutes, until just starting to set. Immediately remove cookies to a wire rack. Spread with frosting when cool. Store in an airtight container. Makes about 2 dozen.

Jasmine Clifton
Colorado Springs, CO

"I created these cookies for my father-in-law, who just loves German chocolate cake. Using cake mix gives you big, soft cookies that are so good!"

—Jasmine

# Snickerdoodles

1 c. margarine, softened
1½ c. plus 3 T. sugar, divided
2 eggs
2¾ c. all-purpose flour

2 t. cream of tartar
1 t. baking soda
½ t. salt
2 t. cinnamon

Blend together margarine, 1½ cups sugar and eggs; add flour, cream of tartar, baking soda and salt. Mix well; chill one hour. Combine remaining sugar and cinnamon in a small bowl; set aside. Shape dough into balls; roll in sugar mixture. Arrange on ungreased baking sheets; bake at 400 degrees for 9 to 10 minutes. Cool for 2 minutes before removing from baking sheets. Makes 3 to 4 dozen.

Tina Knotts
Gooseberry Patch

## Soft + Chewy Pineapple Cookies

2 c. all-purpose flour
1½ c. sugar
½ c. shortening
½ c. canned crushed pineapple

2 eggs, beaten
1 t. baking powder
½ t. baking soda
½ t. salt

Mix all ingredients in a large bowl. Drop dough balls the size of an egg on ungreased baking sheets. Bake at 350 degrees for 12 to 14 minutes, until tops are lightly golden. Makes 3 to 4 dozen.

Carolyn Cochran
Dresden, OH

### toss-ins for a twist

Super-simple ice-cream sandwiches! Place a scoop of softened ice cream on the bottom of one cookie. Top with another cookie, bottom-side down; press together gently. Serve immediately, or wrap and freeze for up to one week.

# Granny's Chocolate Fudge Cookies

Karen Adams (Cincinnati, OH)

14-oz. can sweetened condensed milk

12-oz. pkg. semi-sweet chocolate chips

¼ c. butter

1 c. all-purpose flour

1 c. chopped nuts

1 t. vanilla extract

Place condensed milk, chocolate chips and butter in a microwave-safe bowl. Microwave, uncovered, on high, stirring every 30 seconds, until melted. Add flour, nuts and vanilla. Drop by teaspoonfuls onto greased baking sheets. Bake at 350 degrees for 7 minutes. Cool on wire racks. Makes 5 to 6 dozen.

White Chocolate-Cranberry Cookies

# White Chocolate-Cranberry Cookies

½ c. butter-flavored shortening
1 c. light brown sugar, packed
¼ c. sugar
3.4-oz. pkg. instant French vanilla pudding mix
½ t. baking soda

1½ t. vanilla extract
2½ c. all-purpose flour
1½ c. white chocolate chips
1 c. dried cranberries
½ c. macadamia nuts, crushed

Blend together shortening, sugars, dry pudding mix, baking soda, vanilla and flour in a large bowl. Fold in remaining ingredients. Drop by tablespoonfuls onto parchment paper-lined baking sheets. Bake at 375 degrees for 8 minutes. Makes about 3½ dozen.

Lea Burwell
Charles Town, WV

*"This is a family favorite...even Grandma can't resist eating one of these mouthwatering cookies!"*

*—Lea*

# German Butter Cookies

1 c. plus 1 T. butter
1½ c. sugar
1 t. vanilla extract

1 egg
3 c. all-purpose flour
1 t. baking powder

Melt butter in a saucepan, stirring constantly until golden. Pour butter into a mixing bowl; add sugar, vanilla and egg. Whip until mixture turns nearly white in color. In a separate bowl, sift together flour and baking powder; gradually add to butter mixture. Turn dough onto a flat surface; knead several times. Divide dough in half; form each half into 2 (12-inch) rolls. Chill rolls one hour; cut into ⅜-inch cookie slices. Place slices on ungreased baking sheets; bake at 325 degrees for 16 minutes. Makes about 3 dozen.

Norma Maiwald
Lohrville, IA

*"For a chocolatey treat, dip half of each German Butter Cookie in melted chocolate...yum!"*

*—Norma*

# Sour Cream Drop Cookies

¾ c. butter, softened
1½ c. sugar
2 eggs, beaten
1 t. vanilla extract
½ t. lemon or orange extract

8-oz. container sour cream
3 c. all-purpose flour
1 t. baking powder
1 t. baking soda

Blend butter and sugar in a large bowl. Add eggs, vanilla and lemon or orange extract; mix well. Fold in sour cream; set aside. Combine remaining ingredients in a separate bowl; gradually add to butter mixture. Drop by teaspoonfuls onto greased baking sheets. Bake at 350 degrees for 10 to 12 minutes. Makes 3 dozen.

Cheryl Bastian
Northumberland, PA

# Soft Sugar Cookies

*Oh-so soft. . .just what a sugar cookie should be.*

1 c. shortening
2 c. sugar
2 eggs
2 t. vanilla extract
2 t. baking powder

1 t. baking soda
1 t. salt
4 c. all-purpose flour
1 c. milk
powdered sugar

Beat together shortening and sugar. Add eggs and vanilla; set aside. In a separate bowl, combine baking powder, baking soda, salt and flour; add to shortening mixture alternately with milk, beating well. Chill dough one to 2 hours. Drop by teaspoonfuls into powdered sugar and roll into balls. Place on greased baking sheets. Bake at 350 degrees for 8 to 10 minutes. Makes 4 to 5 dozen.

Dayna Hale
Galena, OH

# Pumpkin Spice Bars

18¼-oz. pkg. spice cake mix
½ c. plus 1 T. butter, melted
   and divided
½ c. pecans, finely chopped
1 T. plus 1 t. vanilla extract,
   divided
8-oz. pkg. cream cheese,
   softened
⅓ c. light brown sugar,
   packed

1 c. canned pumpkin
1 egg
½ c. white chocolate, finely
   chopped
⅓ c. long-cooking oats,
   uncooked
Optional: powdered sugar

Combine cake mix, ½ cup melted butter, pecans and one tablespoon vanilla in a large bowl, mixing well with a fork. Reserve one cup crumbs for streusel topping. Press remaining crumbs into a lightly greased 13"x9" baking pan. Bake at 350 degrees for 13 to 15 minutes, until puffy and set. Cool in pan on a wire rack 20 minutes. Beat cream cheese with an electric mixer at medium speed 30 seconds, or until creamy. Add brown sugar, pumpkin, egg and remaining one teaspoon vanilla; beat until blended. Pour filling over baked crust. Stir white chocolate, remaining one tablespoon melted butter and oats into reserved one cup streusel. Sprinkle over filling. Bake at 350 degrees for 30 minutes, or until edges begin to brown and center is set. Cool completely in pan on a wire rack. Sprinkle with powdered sugar, if desired. Cut into bars. Serve at room temperature or chilled. Makes 2 dozen.

## toss-ins for a twist

If you don't have pecans on hand, you can also use finely chopped walnuts in this fall favorite.

## Raspberry Bars

1 c. butter, softened
¾ c. sugar
1 egg
½ t. vanilla extract
2½ c. all-purpose flour
10-oz. jar seedless
   raspberry jam
½ c. chopped pecans, toasted

Beat butter and sugar in a large bowl until creamy. Add egg and vanilla, beating until blended. Add flour, beating until blended. Reserving one cup dough, press remaining dough firmly into a lightly greased 9"x9" baking pan. Spread jam evenly over crust. Stir pecans into reserved dough. Sprinkle evenly over jam layer. Bake at 350 degrees for 25 to 28 minutes, until golden. Cool completely in pan on a wire rack. Cut into bars. Makes about 1½ dozen.

Vickie
Gooseberry Patch

# Lemon-Coconut Bars

2 c. all-purpose flour
1 c. powdered sugar, divided
1 c. butter, softened
½ c. slivered almonds,
   chopped and toasted
1 c. sweetened flaked coconut

Combine flour and ½ cup powdered sugar in a bowl. Cut butter into flour mixture with a pastry blender or fork until crumbly; stir in almonds. Firmly press mixture into a lightly greased 13"x9" baking pan. Bake at 350 degrees for 20 to 25 minutes, until light golden. Stir coconut into Lemon Chess Pie Filling; pour over baked crust. Bake at 350 degrees for 30 to 35 minutes, until set. Cool in pan on a wire rack. Sprinkle with remaining ½ cup powdered sugar; cut into bars. Makes 32.

# Lemon Chess Pie Filling:

2 c. sugar
4 eggs
¼ c. butter, melted
¼ c. milk
¼ c. lemon juice
1 T. lemon zest
1 T. all-purpose flour
1 T. cornmeal
¼ t. salt

Whisk together all ingredients in a large bowl. Use filling immediately. Makes about 3 cups.

# Angel Bars

16-oz. pkg. angel food
   cake mix
22-oz. can lemon pie filling
1 c. sweetened flaked coconut
   or chopped walnuts
Garnish: powdered sugar

Mix together all ingredients except powdered sugar in a large bowl. Spread in a 13"x9" baking pan that has been greased on the bottom only. Bake at 350 degrees for 25 to 30 minutes. Sift powdered sugar over top while still warm; cut into bars. Makes 16.

Paula Spadaccini
Shelburne, VT

# Caramel-Fudge Brownies

"This recipe came from my very special mother-in-law, and although she's no longer with us, her recipe continues to be a family favorite."

—Sue

18¼-oz. pkg. German chocolate cake mix
¾ c. butter, melted
5-oz. can evaporated milk, divided

14-oz. pkg. caramels, unwrapped
1 c. semi-sweet chocolate chips

Combine cake mix, butter and ⅓ cup evaporated milk in a bowl. Spread half of mixture in a greased 13"x9" baking pan (this layer will be very thin). Bake at 350 degrees for 12 minutes. Place caramels and remaining evaporated milk in a microwave-safe bowl. Microwave, uncovered, on high 3 minutes; stir and set aside. Immediately after removing from oven, sprinkle brownies with chocolate chips; pour caramel mixture over top. Spoon remaining cake batter by heaping tablespoonfuls over caramel layer; do not mix. Bake at 350 degrees for 15 to 17 minutes. Cool completely in pan on a wire rack. Cut into bars. Makes 2 dozen.

Sue Roberson
Peoria, AZ

# The Easiest Brownies Ever

*No bake sale is complete without brownies! Before adding the brownie batter, line your baking pan with aluminum foil and grease the foil. Once the brownies have baked and cooled, they'll lift right out of the pan.*

2 c. milk
3.9-oz. pkg. instant chocolate pudding mix
18¼-oz. pkg. chocolate cake mix

12-oz. pkg. semi-sweet chocolate chips
Garnish: powdered sugar

Combine milk and pudding mix in a large bowl; add cake mix and stir until well blended. Stir in chocolate chips; spread in a greased 15"x10" jelly-roll pan. Bake at 350 degrees for 30 minutes, or until set in the middle. Cool in pan on a wire rack; cut into bars and sprinkle with powdered sugar. Makes 12 to 15.

Tammy Rowe
Bellevue, OH

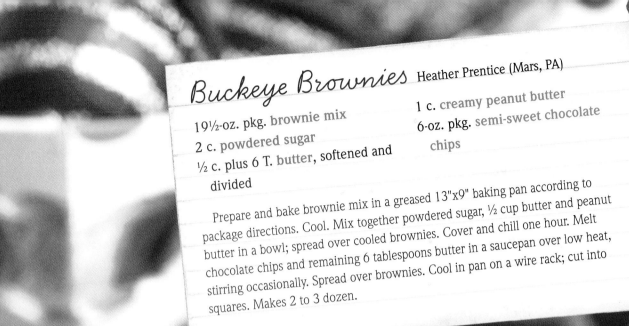

# Buckeye Brownies
Heather Prentice (Mars, PA)

19½-oz. pkg. brownie mix
2 c. powdered sugar
½ c. plus 6 T. butter, softened and
  divided

1 c. creamy peanut butter
6-oz. pkg. semi-sweet chocolate
  chips

Prepare and bake brownie mix in a greased 13"x9" baking pan according to package directions. Cool. Mix together powdered sugar, ½ cup butter and peanut butter in a bowl; spread over cooled brownies. Cover and chill one hour. Melt chocolate chips and remaining 6 tablespoons butter in a saucepan over low heat, stirring occasionally. Spread over brownies. Cool in pan on a wire rack; cut into squares. Makes 2 to 3 dozen.

# Soda Shoppe Chocolate Malts

*Good, old-fashioned fun!*

8 scoops vanilla ice cream
3 c. milk
¼ c. malted milk powder
4 to 6 T. chocolate syrup
2 t. vanilla extract

Combine all ingredients in a blender. Cover and process until smooth and well blended. Serve immediately. Serves 4.

Jill Burton
Gooseberry Patch

## supper in a snap

Everyone loves dessert! For a fast and fun treat on a busy weeknight, put out all the ingredients for these super sweets and let everyone make their own.

# Skyscraper Banana Splits

*Big and little kids will line up for these!*

¼ c. chocolate syrup
4 scoops vanilla ice cream
4 bananas, halved lengthwise and crosswise
4 scoops chocolate ice cream
½ c. strawberry syrup
Garnish: whipped cream, maraschino cherries

Pour chocolate syrup into 4 parfait glasses; add vanilla ice cream to each. Arrange banana pieces, cut-side out, in glasses; top with chocolate ice cream. Drizzle with strawberry syrup; top with whipped cream and cherries. Serves 4.

Beth Kramer
Port Saint Lucie, FL

Skyscraper
Banana Splits

Soda Shoppe
Chocolate Malts

# Bread Pudding

*Day-old bread is best for soaking up the liquid in this oh-so decadent dessert.*

4 eggs
1½ c. sugar
3 12-oz. cans evaporated milk
½ c. butter, melted
1 T. vanilla extract
2 t. cinnamon
6 c. French bread, torn into
  pieces and packed

1 Granny Smith apple, peeled,
  cored and chopped
1½ c. walnuts, coarsely
  chopped and toasted
1 c. golden raisins

Beat eggs with a whisk in a large bowl. Whisk in sugar, evaporated milk, melted butter, vanilla and cinnamon. Fold in bread, apple, walnuts and raisins, stirring until bread is moistened. Pour into a greased 13"x9" baking pan. Bake, uncovered, at 350 degrees for 50 minutes, or until set. Cut into squares. Serve warm with Rum Sauce. Serves 12.

## Rum Sauce:

2 14-oz. cans sweetened
  condensed milk
2 T. dark rum or 1 t. rum
  extract

1 T. vanilla extract

Pour condensed milk into a small saucepan; cook over medium heat until hot, stirring often. Remove from heat; stir in rum and vanilla. Serve warm. Makes 2½ cups.

# Mom Gowdy's Ambrosia

*Ambrosia looks so pretty when served in clear glass dessert cups.*

2 20-oz. cans pineapple
  chunks, drained
2 11-oz. cans mandarin
  oranges, drained

2 c. mini marshmallows
2 c. sour cream
1 c. sweetened flaked coconut

Mix all ingredients in a serving bowl; cover and refrigerate. Serves
8 to 10.

Linda Day
Wall Township, NJ

# Supreme Cheesecake Dip

*Make the serving bowl for this dip kid friendly and fun.*

2 8-oz. pkgs. cream cheese,
  softened
½ c. frozen strawberries,
  thawed and drained
¼ c. sugar

¼ c. sour cream
1½ t. vanilla extract
graham crackers
fresh fruit

Combine cream cheese, strawberries, sugar, sour cream and vanilla in
a blender. Cover and blend until very smooth; chill at least 2 hours. Serve
with graham crackers and fresh fruit for dipping. Makes about 3 cups.

Patricia Walker
Mocksville, NC

# Frosty Butter Pecan Crunch Pie

2 c. graham cracker crumbs
½ c. butter, melted
2 3.4-oz. pkgs. instant vanilla
  pudding mix
2 c. milk
1 qt. butter pecan ice cream,
  slightly softened

8-oz. container frozen
  whipped topping, thawed
2 1.4-oz. chocolate-covered
  toffee candy bars, crushed

Combine graham cracker crumbs and melted butter in a medium bowl; pat into an ungreased 13"x9" baking pan. Freeze until firm. Beat pudding mix and milk in a large bowl with an electric mixer at medium speed until well blended, about one minute. Fold in ice cream and whipped topping; spoon over chilled crust. Sprinkle with crushed candy bars; cover and freeze. Remove from freezer 20 minutes before serving. Serves 12 to 15.

Lisa Johnson
Hallsville, TX

# No-Bake Cherry Cheesecake

"Whenever I make this dessert, I know my little six-year-old neighbor will come running. It's a favorite in our family too. It's so easy to make...and you don't even have to turn on the oven!"

–Janet

8-oz. pkg. cream cheese,
  softened
14-oz. can sweetened
  condensed milk

⅓ c. lemon juice
1 t. vanilla extract
9-inch graham cracker crust
21-oz. can cherry pie filling

Beat cream cheese and condensed milk in a bowl until light and fluffy. Add lemon juice and vanilla; stir until well mixed. Pour filling into crust. Cover and chill 3 hours; top with pie filling. Serves 6 to 8.

Janet Parsons
Pickerington, OH

# Mocha-Pecan Mud Pie

*Two store-bought ice creams pack lots of flavor into this frozen pie.*

12 chocolate sandwich
   cookies, crushed
3 T. butter or margarine,
   melted
1 egg white, lightly beaten
1¼ c. chopped pecans
¼ c. sugar
1 pt. coffee ice cream, softened
1 pt. chocolate ice cream,
   softened

12 chocolate sandwich
   cookies, coarsely chopped
   and divided
Optional: frozen whipped
   topping, thawed, additional
   cookies and pecans, coarsely
   chopped

Stir together cookie crumbs and melted butter in a medium bowl. Press into an ungreased 9" pie plate. Brush with egg white. Bake at 350 degrees for 5 minutes. Cool on a wire rack. Place pecans on a lightly greased baking sheet; sprinkle with sugar. Bake at 350 degrees for 8 to 10 minutes. Cool. Stir together ice creams, one cup coarsely chopped cookies and one cup pecans in a bowl; spoon into crust. Freeze 10 minutes. Press remaining coarsely chopped cookies and pecans on top. Cover and freeze at least 8 hours. Garnish with whipped topping and additional chopped cookies and pecans, if desired. Serves 8.

## pies galore

Consider having a Pie Night. Invite family & friends to bring their favorite pie to share. And don't forget copies of the recipes…someone's sure to ask!

# Million-Dollar Pound Cake

2 c. butter, softened
3 c. sugar
6 eggs
4 c. all-purpose flour
¾ c. milk

1 t. almond extract
1 t. vanilla extract
Optional: sweetened whipped cream, blueberries, sliced peaches

Beat butter in a bowl with an electric mixer at medium speed until light yellow in color and creamy. Gradually add sugar, beating at medium speed until light and fluffy. Add eggs, one at a time, beating just until yellow disappears after each addition. Add flour to butter mixture alternately with milk, beginning and ending with flour. Beat at low speed just until blended after each addition. (Batter should be smooth). Stir in extracts. Pour batter into a greased and floured 10" tube pan. Bake at 300 degrees for one hour and 40 minutes, or until a long wooden pick inserted in center comes out clean. Cool in pan on a wire rack 10 to 15 minutes. Remove from pan and cool completely on wire rack. Garnish each serving with whipped cream, blueberries and sliced peaches, if desired. Serves 10 to 12.

# Carrot Cake

1 c. oil
1 t. vanilla extract
4 eggs
2 c. sugar
2 c. all-purpose flour
2 t. baking soda

2 t. baking powder
2 t. cinnamon
1 t. salt
1 c. chopped walnuts
3 c. carrots, grated

Mix together oil, vanilla and eggs in a small bowl; set aside. Combine sugar, flour, baking soda, baking powder, cinnamon and salt in a large bowl; stir in egg mixture. Add nuts and carrots, mixing well. Pour batter into 3 greased and floured 8" round cake pans. Bake layers at 350 degrees for 35 minutes, or until toothpick inserted in center comes out clean. Cool several minutes, remove from pans to wire racks to cool completely. Spread Icing between layers and over top and sides of cake. Serves 8 to 10.

## Icing:

½ c. butter
8-oz. pkg. cream cheese

2 c. powdered sugar

Beat together all ingredients until smooth.

## vintage finds

Look for vintage pie tins, servers and cake plates at flea markets...add them to your collection, or make them part of the gift when sharing a favorite sweet treat.

# Cookies 'n' Cream Cake

18½-oz. pkg. white cake mix
1¼ c. water
⅓ c. oil
1 t. vanilla extract
3 eggs
1 c. chocolate sandwich cookies, crushed

Combine cake mix, water, oil, vanilla and eggs in a large mixing bowl; blend with an electric mixer at low speed just until moistened. Blend at high speed 2 minutes; gently fold in crushed cookies. Line two 8" round cake pans with wax paper; grease and flour pans. Pour batter into pans; bake at 350 degrees for 25 minutes, or until a toothpick inserted in center comes out clean. Cool 10 minutes; remove from pans to a wire rack to cool completely. Spread with Frosting. Serves 12.

## Frosting:

½ c. butter, softened, or shortening
1 t. vanilla extract
4 c. powdered sugar
¼ c. milk

Beat butter and vanilla in a large bowl until creamy. Add powdered sugar and milk alternately to butter mixture, beating until desired consistency. Makes about 4 cups.

Shari Miller
Hobart, IN

*extra special*

For a little something extra on cakes and brownies, try topping with chopped candy bars. Make chopping a breeze when you wrap them in plastic wrap and freeze 10 to 15 minutes beforehand.

# Warm Turtle Cake

18¼-oz. pkg. Swiss chocolate
   cake mix
½ c. plus ⅓ c. evaporated
   milk, divided
¾ c. butter, melted

14-oz. pkg. caramels,
   unwrapped
1 c. chopped pecans
¾ c. chocolate chips

Beat cake mix, ⅓ cup evaporated milk and melted butter in a large bowl with an electric mixer at medium speed 2 minutes. Pour half of batter into a greased 11"x7" baking pan. Bake at 350 degrees for 6 minutes. Melt caramels in the remaining ½ cup evaporated milk in a double boiler over simmering water or in microwave. Stir well; drizzle over cake. Sprinkle pecans and chocolate chips over caramel mixture. Use a wet knife to spread the remaining cake batter over the pecans and chocolate chips. Bake at 350 degrees for 18 minutes. Serves 12.

"A cake that reminds me of the boxes of chocolate-covered turtles that my dad used to bring home for us when we were little!"

–Laurie

Laurie Benham
Playas, NM

# Fresh Strawberry Shortcake

*When time is short, use split biscuits, cubed angel food cake or waffles for a speedy version of strawberry shortcake.*

> "No doubt, one of the best things about summer. Our strawberry patch has become so large that I've shared lots of plants...and this recipe...with all our friends & neighbors!"
>
> —Nancy

1 qt. strawberries, hulled and sliced
1 c. sugar, divided
2 c. all-purpose flour
4 t. baking powder
¼ t. salt
⅛ t. nutmeg
½ c. butter
½ c. milk
2 eggs, separated
2 c. sweetened whipped cream

Gently toss together strawberries and ½ cup sugar in a bowl; cover and chill. Combine flour, ¼ cup sugar, baking powder, salt and nutmeg in a large bowl; cut in butter with a pastry blender or fork until crumbly. Combine milk and egg yolks in a small bowl; mix well. Add to flour mixture, stirring just until moistened. Divide dough in half; pat into 2 greased 9" round cake pans. Beat egg whites in a small bowl with an electric mixer at medium speed until stiff peaks form; spread over dough. Sprinkle with remaining ¼ cup sugar. Bake at 300 degrees for 40 to 45 minutes, until golden. Cool 10 minutes before removing from pans to a wire rack. Cool completely. Place one cake layer on a large serving plate; spread with half the whipped cream. Spoon half the strawberries over cream. Repeat layers.

Nancy Ramsey
Gooseberry Patch

## berry fresh

To keep berries at their sweetest and juiciest, set an ice-filled cooler in the car and tuck baskets of berries inside for the ride home. Keep them refrigerated and use in a favorite recipe within a couple of days.

Grandma & Katie's
Frozen Dessert

# Grandma + Katie's Frozen Dessert

*Refreshing during the summer, or any time of year, this tasty treat can be made ahead of time.*

½ c. creamy peanut butter
½ c. light corn syrup
2 c. crispy rice cereal
2 c. chocolate-flavored crispy rice cereal

½ gal. vanilla ice cream, softened
½ to 1 c. Spanish peanuts, coarsely chopped
Optional: chocolate syrup

Blend together peanut butter and corn syrup in a large bowl. Add cereals; stir until coated. Press into the bottom of an ungreased 13"x9" baking pan. Spread ice cream over cereal mixture; sprinkle with peanuts. Swirl chocolate syrup over top, if desired. Cover with aluminum foil; freeze at least 4 hours before serving. Cut into squares to serve. Serves 15 to 18.

Jennifer Brown
Garden Grove, CA

*"This used to be my favorite birthday cake every year...I loved it! To this day, every time we make this dessert, I think of all those birthday parties in the backyard."*

*—Jennifer*

# Caramel-Marshmallow Delights

10-oz. box crispy rice cereal
14-oz. can sweetened condensed milk
½ c. butter

14-oz. pkg. caramels, unwrapped
16-oz. pkg. marshmallows

Place rice cereal in a large bowl. Combine condensed milk, butter and caramels in a heavy saucepan over medium heat; stir until butter and caramels melt and mixture is smooth. Remove from heat; quickly dip marshmallows into mixture; roll in rice cereal. Arrange on an aluminum foil-lined baking sheet; refrigerate 30 minutes. Remove from baking sheet; store in an airtight container in refrigerator. Makes 5 to 6 dozen.

Shelley Haverkate
Grandville, MI

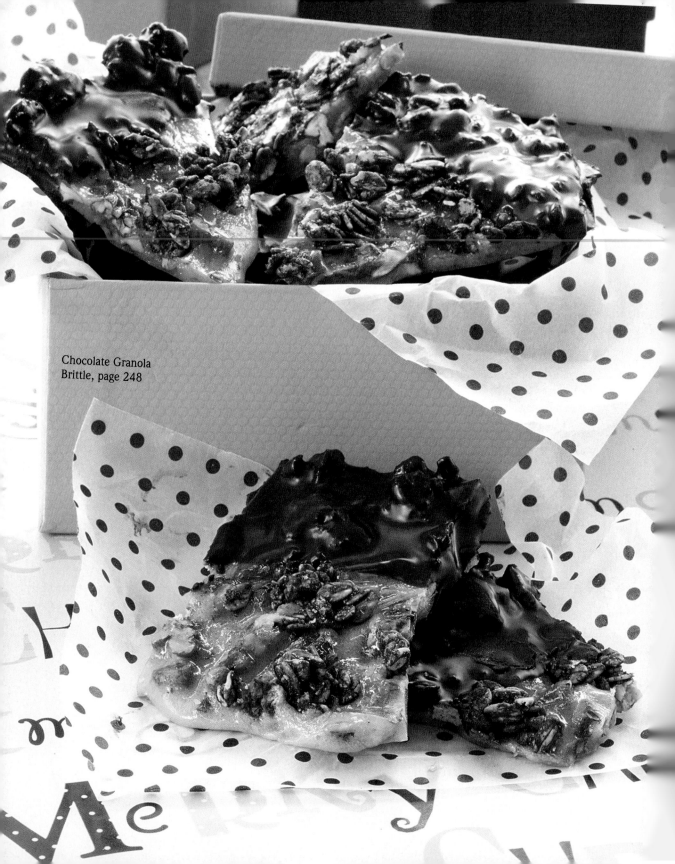

Chocolate Granola
Brittle, page 248

# festive celebrations

A holiday get-together wouldn't be complete without tasty appetizers, main dishes and yummy desserts! Heading to a New Year's Eve party? Bring along some Holiday Ham Balls or Chocolate Chess Pie. Celebrate the Fourth of July with Corn Dogs. No matter what time of year you serve them, these festive dishes will be a hit!

# Holiday Ham Balls

*A family favorite for years. Good for breakfast too. Mix up ingredients the night before and refrigerate…they'll be ready to bake when you get up.*

3 c. biscuit baking mix
1½ c. smoked ham, finely chopped
16-oz. pkg. shredded Cheddar cheese

⅔ c. milk
½ c. grated Parmesan cheese
2 T. dried parsley
2 t. spicy mustard

Mix all ingredients thoroughly in a large bowl; shape into one-inch balls. Place about 2 inches apart on lightly greased 15"x10" jelly-roll pans. Bake at 350 degrees for 20 to 25 minutes, until lightly golden. Remove from pans immediately; serve warm. Makes 7 dozen.

Jeanette Lawrence
Vacaville, CA

## winter blooms

Enjoy a springtime bouquet during winter's frosty days! Fill a galvanized pail with pebbles, and tuck in a variety of tulip, daffodil or hyacinth bulbs. Add just enough water to barely cover the pebbles. Keep watered, and in a few weeks you'll have lots of springtime blossoms.

# Jo Ann's Holiday Brie

*One of my favorite holiday recipes…great for "pop-in" guests because it's so quick & easy to prepare.*

13.2-oz. pkg. Brie cheese
¼ c. caramel ice-cream
   topping
½ c. sweetened dried
   cranberries

½ c. dried apricots, chopped
½ c. chopped pecans
assorted crackers

Place Brie on an ungreased microwave-safe dish; microwave, uncovered, on high 10 to 15 seconds. Cut out a wedge to see if center is soft. If center is still firm, microwave cheese an additional 5 to 10 seconds, until cheese is soft and spreadable. Watch carefully, as the center will begin to melt quickly. Drizzle with caramel topping; sprinkle with cranberries, apricots and nuts. Serve with crackers. Serves 6 to 8.

Jo Ann
Gooseberry Patch

Garden-Fresh
Egg Casserole

# Garden-Fresh Egg Casserole

*Fresh tomatoes and spinach turn this breakfast casserole into something extra special!*

18 eggs, beaten
1½ c. shredded Monterey
   Jack cheese
1 c. spinach, chopped
1 c. tomatoes, chopped
1 c. cottage cheese
1 c. buttermilk
½ c. butter, melted
½ c. onion, grated

Combine all ingredients in a large bowl; pour into a greased 13"x9" baking pan. Cover; refrigerate overnight. Bake, uncovered, at 350 degrees for 50 minutes to one hour. Serves 8 to 10.

Anne Muns
Scottsdale, AZ

# Christmas Morning Chile Relleno

*Serve with fruit salad and sausage links for a spicy Christmas breakfast.*

16-oz. pkg. shredded Cheddar
   cheese
16-oz. pkg. shredded Monterey
   Jack cheese
2 4-oz. cans chopped green
   chiles
4 eggs
1 c. evaporated milk
¼ c. all-purpose flour

Sprinkle cheeses and chiles alternately in a greased 13"x9" baking pan. Whisk together eggs, milk and flour in a medium bowl and pour over cheese mixture. Bake, uncovered, at 350 degrees for 30 minutes. Cool slightly before serving. Serves 8 to 10.

Angela Leikem
Silverton, OR

## toss-ins for a twist

Serve this zippy breakfast dish alongside salsa, sour cream, jalapeño peppers and cilantro for added flavor.

# Herbed Roast Turkey Breast

*This is too good to serve only once or twice a year!*

4 to 5-lb turkey breast
¼ c. fresh parsley, chopped
1 T. fresh thyme or rosemary,
   chopped
zest and juice of 1 lemon
2 tart apples, peeled, cored and
   chopped

2 stalks celery, cut into thirds
4 shallots, coarsely chopped
1 c. chicken broth
½ c. dry white wine or
   chicken broth
2 T. butter, melted
2 T. all-purpose flour

Separate skin from turkey breast with your fingers to make a pocket. Combine herbs and lemon zest in a small bowl; rub under skin. Pat skin back into place. Place apples, celery, shallots, broth and wine or broth in a 4-quart slow cooker. Place turkey skin-side up on top; drizzle lemon juice over turkey. Cover and cook on high setting for 3½ to 4 hours or on low setting for 8 to 10 hours, until tender. Remove turkey from slow cooker; if desired, place in a preheated 450-degree oven 5 to 10 minutes, until skin is golden. Transfer turkey to a serving platter and keep warm. Discard apples and celery from slow cooker; pour drippings into a skillet over medium heat. Combine butter and flour in a small bowl. Whisk into drippings; cook and stir about 15 minutes, or until thickened and bubbly. Serve warm gravy with sliced turkey. Serves 4 to 6.

Robin Lakin
La Palma, CA

# Deep-Fried Turkey

*Fried turkey is incredibly moist, succulent and, amazingly, has no greasy taste!*

12 to 15-lb. turkey
Optional: 2 T. cayenne pepper
4 to 5 gal. peanut oil

Optional: fresh sage, parsley and thyme sprigs, kumquats with leaves

Remove giblets and neck from turkey; rinse turkey with cold water. Drain cavity well; pat dry. Place turkey on fryer rod; allow all liquid to drain from cavity (20 to 30 minutes). Rub outside of turkey with cayenne pepper, if desired. Pour oil into a deep propane turkey fryer 10 to 12 inches from top; heat to 375 degrees over a medium-low flame according to manufacturer's instructions. Carefully lower turkey into hot oil with rod attachment. (Keep oil temperature at 340 degrees.) Fry 55 minutes, or until a meat thermometer inserted in turkey breast registers 165 degrees. Remove turkey from oil; drain and let stand 15 minutes before slicing. Garnish with sage, parsley and thyme sprigs and kumquats, if desired. Serves 20.

## supper in a snap

This 12 to 15-lb. turkey should make enough for leftovers. Use it to make sandwiches or an after-Thanksgiving pizza.

## kids' table

Make the kids' table fun! Use a sheet of butcher paper for the tablecloth; place a flowerpot filled with markers, crayons and stickers in the middle...they'll have a blast!

# Whole Baked Ham

*A yummy ham that can be served hot or refrigerated and sliced for biscuits.*

12 to 14-lb. fully cooked
    boneless or bone-in ham
12 whole cloves
1½ c. pineapple juice
½ c. maple-flavored syrup

6 slices canned pineapple
1 c. water
¾ c. brown sugar, packed
3 T. mustard

Place ham, fat-side up, in an ungreased shallow roasting pan. Press cloves into top of ham. Stir together pineapple juice and syrup in a bowl; pour over ham. Arrange pineapple slices on ham. Bake at 325 degrees for 1½ hours. Add water and bake 1½ more hours. Remove from oven; remove pineapple slices. Mix together brown sugar and mustard in a small bowl; spread over ham. Bake 30 more minutes. Serves 18 to 20.

Jacqueline Kurtz
Reading, PA

## flea market finds

Keep an eye open at flea markets and tag sales for jelly molds and cake tins...dressed up with cellophane and ribbon, they're ideal for holding holiday treats to share.

# Pork & Raspberry Sauce

*A tender pork roast will make your family's holiday homecoming so memorable!*

3 to 4-lb. boneless pork loin
  roast
1 t. salt

1 t. pepper
1 t. rubbed sage

Sprinkle roast with salt, pepper and sage. Place roast on an ungreased rack in a shallow roasting pan. Bake at 325 degrees for 1½ to 2 hours, until meat thermometer registers 150 degrees. Cover and let stand until thermometer registers 160 degrees. Place roast on platter; serve with Raspberry Sauce. Serves 10.

## Raspberry Sauce:

12-oz. pkg. frozen raspberries,
  thawed
3 c. sugar
½ c. white vinegar
½ t. ground cloves
½ t. ground ginger

½ t. nutmeg
½ c. cornstarch
2 T. lemon juice
2 T. butter, melted
6 to 8 drops red food coloring

Drain raspberries, reserving juice. Add water to juice, if necessary, to make 1½ cups. Combine one cup of the raspberry liquid with sugar, vinegar, cloves, ginger and nutmeg in a saucepan. Bring to a boil. Reduce heat; simmer, uncovered, 10 minutes. Blend cornstarch and remaining ½ cup raspberry liquid in a small bowl; add to saucepan. Cook over medium heat, stirring constantly, one minute, or until thickened. Stir in raspberries, lemon juice, butter and food coloring.

Robbin Chamberlain
Worthington, OH

## toss-ins for a twist

Substitute cranberries for the raspberries in the sauce for this pork loin.

# Corn Dogs

1 c. all-purpose flour
2 T. sugar
1½ t. baking powder
1 t. salt
⅔ c. cornmeal
2 T. shortening

1 egg
¾ c. milk
8 to 10 hot dogs
8 to 10 wooden sticks
oil for deep frying

## toss-ins for a twist

Give Corn Dogs a new spin by using Italian sausage or bratwurst instead of hot dogs.

Combine flour, sugar, baking powder and salt in a medium bowl; stir in cornmeal. Using a pastry blender or 2 forks, cut in shortening until crumbly; set aside. Blend together egg and milk in a separate bowl. Stir into cornmeal mixture. Thoroughly dry each hot dog with a paper towel to ensure batter will cling. Insert a stick into each; dip in batter. Pour oil to a depth of 2 to 3 inches in a deep fryer; heat oil to 350 to 375 degrees. Fry corn dogs in hot oil 4 to 5 minutes, until golden. Serves 8 to 10.

Kay Marone
Des Moines, IA

# Garlicky Baked Shrimp

*Here's the perfect party recipe...guests peel their own shrimp and save you the work! To bake this when you're on vacation, purchase a large disposable roasting pan for easy clean-up. French bread is perfect to sop up the savory sauce.*

2 lbs. uncooked large shrimp,
   cleaned and unpeeled
16-oz. bottle Italian salad
   dressing
1½ T. pepper

2 cloves garlic, pressed
2 lemons, halved
¼ c. fresh parsley, chopped
½ c. butter, cut into pieces

Place shrimp, salad dressing, pepper and garlic in an ungreased 13"x9" baking pan, tossing to coat. Squeeze juice from lemons over shrimp mixture and stir. Cut lemon halves into wedges and add to pan. Sprinkle shrimp with parsley; dot with butter. Bake, uncovered, at 375 degrees for 25 minutes, stirring after 15 minutes. Serve in pan. Serves 6.

# Grandma's Holiday Stuffing

*Apples keep this stuffing moist.*

1 large loaf day-old bread, torn
Optional: day-old corn muffins,
   broken into pieces
½ c. butter
1 onion, diced
3 stalks celery, diced
Optional: ½ c. sliced
   mushrooms

2 tart apples, cored and diced
½ c. walnuts, coarsely
   chopped
½ c. raisins
½ to ¾ c. water
½ to 1 T. poultry seasoning
dried parsley to taste
salt and pepper to taste

Place torn bread in an ungreased large baking pan; mix in muffin pieces, if using. Bake at 250 degrees for 30 minutes, or until dried out. Set aside. Melt butter in a large skillet over low heat; sauté onion, celery and mushrooms, if using, until tender. Add apples, walnuts and raisins; stir to coat with butter. Mix in water and seasonings; pour over bread and toss to moisten. Add a little more water if bread is very dry. Use to stuff a 12 to 15-pound turkey before roasting; do not overstuff. Or spread stuffing in a lightly greased 9"x5" loaf pan and bake at 350 degrees for 30 to 40 minutes. Serves 8 to 10.

Wendy Lee Paffenroth
Pine Island, NY

## toss-ins for a twist

Also consider adding a sleeve of saltine crackers to the holiday stuffing in place of the day-old corn muffins.

# Aunt Fanny's Baked Squash

*A flavorful side dish for holiday get-togethers or church suppers.*

### supper in a snap

You can prepare this dish ahead of time, refrigerate and bake just before serving to make the Christmas meal easier.

3 lbs. **yellow squash**, cubed, cooked and mashed
¼ c. **butter**, softened
2 **eggs**, beaten
½ c. **onion**, chopped

1 T. **sugar**
1 t. **salt**
½ t. **pepper**
¾ c. **bread crumbs**, divided
¼ c. **butter**, melted

Combine squash, softened butter, eggs, onion, sugar, salt and pepper in a large bowl; mix well. Stir in ¼ cup bread crumbs. Spoon squash mixture into a greased 2-quart casserole dish; set aside. Combine remaining ½ cup bread crumbs and melted butter in a small bowl; toss lightly. Sprinkle crumbs over squash mixture. Bake, uncovered, at 375 degrees for one hour. Serves 8 to 10.

Ginger Parsons
Lynchburg, VA

# Waldorf Slaw

*Everyone will love this tangy salad that's easily made ahead.*

16-oz. pkg. coleslaw mix
2 c. Braeburn apples, peeled,
  cored and chopped
1 c. Bartlett pears, peeled,
  cored and chopped
½ c. raisins
3 T. chopped walnuts

½ c. mayonnaise
½ c. buttermilk
1 t. lemon zest
2 T. lemon juice
¼ t. salt
⅛ t. pepper

Combine coleslaw, apples, pears, raisins and walnuts in a large bowl; set aside. Combine remaining ingredients in a separate bowl, stirring well with a whisk. Drizzle mayonnaise mixture over coleslaw mixture and toss to coat. Cover and refrigerate 30 minutes. Serves 10.

Lori Rosenberg
University Heights, OH

# Spinach Salad + Hot Bacon Dressing

*The hot & savory dressing is the key ingredient to this salad's fantastic taste.*

10-oz. bag spinach, torn into
  bite-size pieces
4 eggs, hard-boiled, peeled and
  sliced
1 tomato, chopped
1 red onion, sliced
8 to 10 large mushrooms,
  sliced

Toss together all ingredients in a large bowl; serve with Hot Bacon Dressing. Serves 4.

## Hot Bacon Dressing:

1 lb. bacon, cut into 1-inch
  pieces
1 onion, chopped
1 clove garlic, minced
½ c. brown sugar, packed
½ c. red wine vinegar
2 c. water, divided
½ t. pepper
¼ t. salt
1 T. cornstarch

Sauté bacon, onion and garlic in a large skillet over medium heat until bacon is crisp. Add brown sugar, vinegar, 1½ cups water, pepper and salt; simmer until mixture is reduced by half. Mix together cornstarch and remaining ½ cup water in a bowl; add to pan and simmer until thick and bubbly. Makes 2 cups.

Kristie Rigo
Friedens, PA

# Hoppin' John

1 c. dried black-eyed peas
10 c. water, divided
6 slices bacon, coarsely chopped
¾ c. green onions, chopped
1 stalk celery, chopped
1½ t. salt
¾ t. cayenne pepper
1 c. long-cooking rice, uncooked

Rinse peas and place in a large saucepan with 6 cups water. Bring to a boil; reduce heat and simmer 2 minutes. Remove from heat, cover and let stand one hour. Drain and rinse. Cook bacon in the same pan over medium heat until crisp. Drain off drippings, reserving 3 tablespoons in pan. Add peas, remaining 4 cups water, green onions, celery, salt and cayenne pepper. Bring to a boil, cover and reduce heat. Simmer 30 minutes. Add rice; cover and simmer 20 more minutes, or until peas and rice are tender. Serves 4 to 6.

Green Bean
Bundles

# Green Bean Bundles

*Easy and delicious! The most obvious time-saver in this recipe is to skip making the bundles, but it is definitely worth the effort.*

3 14½-oz. cans whole green
   beans, drained
8 slices bacon, cut in half
   crosswise

6 T. butter, melted
½ c. brown sugar, packed
2 to 3 cloves garlic, minced

Gather beans into bundles of 10; wrap each bundle with a half-slice of bacon. Arrange bundles in a lightly greased 13"x9" baking pan. Mix melted butter, brown sugar and garlic in a small bowl; spoon over bundles. Cover and bake at 375 degrees for 30 minutes. Uncover and bake 15 more minutes. Serves 8.

Wendy Sensing
Brentwood, TN

# Gerry's Green Bean Bake

4 c. green beans, trimmed and
   sliced
1 onion, finely chopped
¼ c. plus 3 T. butter, melted
   and divided

1 c. sour cream
2 T. lemon juice
salt and pepper to taste
½ c. saltine crackers, crushed

Cover green beans with water in a large saucepan. Cook over medium heat about 15 minutes, just until tender; drain. Meanwhile, sauté onion in ¼ cup butter in a small saucepan over medium heat until tender. Mix together green beans, sour cream, lemon juice, sautéed onion, salt and pepper in a bowl. Transfer to a buttered 2-quart casserole dish. Mix together crackers and remaining 3 tablespoons butter in a small bowl. Sprinkle over green bean mixture. Bake, uncovered, at 375 degrees for 20 minutes. Serves 6.

Teresa Amert
Upper Sandusky, OH

*"This recipe came from my sister, Gerry, who is an excellent cook. The sour cream and lemon juice make this casserole delicious."*

*—Teresa*

# All-American Summer Slaw

16-oz. pkg. coleslaw mix
1½ c. sweetened dried
  cranberries
½ c. sliced almonds, toasted
½ c. celery, diced

½ c. red pepper, diced
¼ c. green onions, sliced
1 c. honey mustard salad
  dressing

Combine all ingredients except salad dressing in a large bowl; mix well. Pour dressing over slaw mixture; stir well. Cover and refrigerate until ready to serve. Mix well before serving. Serves 4 to 6.

Julie Horn
Chrisney, IN

# Stovetop Baked Beans

*A simple way to give canned pork & beans a little pizazz.*

3 15-oz. cans pork & beans
1 to 2 T. brown sugar, packed
2 T. barbecue sauce

1 T. mustard
¼ lb. bacon, chopped

Mix all ingredients except bacon in a saucepan. Simmer over medium heat. Meanwhile, cook bacon in a skillet over medium heat until crisp. Drain bacon and stir into bean mixture. Reduce heat to low and continue to simmer 15 minutes, stirring occasionally. Serves 6.

Bob Poerio
Munster, IN

Stovetop
Baked Beans

All-American
Summer Slaw

Country Butterscotch Yams

# Country Butterscotch Yams

*For an extra treat, top with half of a 16-ounce package of marshmallows and return to the oven until lightly browned.*

8 14-oz. cans yams, peeled, cut
    into ½-inch slices and boiled
½ c. brown sugar, packed
½ c. corn syrup

¼ c. half-and-half
2 T. butter
½ t. salt
½ t. cinnamon

Arrange yams in an ungreased 13"x9" baking pan; bake, uncovered, at 325 degrees for 15 minutes. Combine remaining ingredients in a 2-quart saucepan; boil 5 minutes, stirring constantly. Pour over yams; bake, uncovered, 15 more minutes, basting often. Serves 6.

Charlotte Weaver
Purcell, OK

# German Hot Potato Salad

6 slices bacon, finely chopped
1 onion, sliced
½ c. water
⅓ c. vinegar
1 T. sugar
2 t. all-purpose flour

1½ t. salt
¼ t. pepper
½ c. fresh parsley, chopped
1¼ lbs. potatoes, peeled, sliced
    and cooked

Sauté bacon in a large skillet over medium heat until crisp. Drain off most of the drippings; add onion to drippings in skillet and sauté 2 minutes. Add remaining ingredients except potatoes; cook and stir until thickened. Add potatoes and stir well. Serve warm. Serves 4 to 6.

Jennifer Savino
Joliet, IL

*"My grandma was famous for this recipe...she'd bring a huge bowl to share at every family or community occasion. Definitely a comfort food and so delicious!"*

*—Jennifer*

# Golden Potato Latkes

*Enjoy these tasty potato pancakes the traditional way…topped with applesauce and a dollop of sour cream.*

4 potatoes, peeled
1 onion, peeled and quartered
¼ c. all-purpose flour
4 eggs, beaten

1 t. salt
½ t. pepper
¾ c. olive oil

Shred potatoes and onion in a food processor; transfer to a large bowl. Stir in flour, eggs, salt and pepper until blended. Heat oil in a large skillet over medium-high heat. Drop potato mixture into hot oil, 2 tablespoons at a time. Cook over medium-high heat, turning once, until golden. Drain on paper towels; serve warm. Makes about 4 dozen.

Irene Robinson
Cincinnati, OH

# Double-Cheese Scalloped Potatoes

*Two kinds of cheese make these potatoes a treat!*

### toss-ins for a twist

Add a dash of cayenne pepper to add a touch of flavor to this tasty potato dish.

5 c. potatoes, peeled, sliced
  and cooked
2 c. small-curd cottage cheese
1½ c. sour cream

½ c. onion, chopped
½ t. salt
½ t. garlic salt
1 c. shredded Cheddar cheese

Mix all ingredients except Cheddar cheese in a large bowl; pour into a greased 13"x9" baking pan. Sprinkle with Cheddar cheese; bake, uncovered, at 350 degrees for 30 to 40 minutes. Serves 12.

Rogene Rogers
Bemidji, MN

Double-Cheese
Scalloped Potatoes

# Chocolate Bread

*make-ahead magic*

Make this bread up to a month in advance and freeze it. Wrap it in brown kraft paper tied with festive holiday ribbon to give to family and friends.

1¼ c. milk
½ c. water
1 env. active dry yeast
4½ c. all-purpose flour, divided
½ c. baking cocoa
¼ c. sugar

1 t. salt
1 egg
2 T. butter, softened
8 1-oz. sqs. semi-sweet baking chocolate, chopped
1½ T. turbinado sugar

Heat milk and water until very warm, about 110 to 115 degrees. Combine with yeast in a large bowl; whisk until smooth. Let stand 5 minutes. Stir 2 cups flour, cocoa, sugar and salt into yeast mixture; beat with an electric mixer at medium speed until smooth. Beat in egg, butter and 2 cups flour until a soft dough forms. Turn dough out onto a floured surface; knead until smooth (about 6 minutes), adding remaining ½ cup flour, one tablespoon at a time, as needed to prevent dough from sticking. Fold in chopped chocolate during last minute of kneading. Place dough in a large, lightly greased bowl, turning to coat top. Cover with plastic wrap; let rise in a warm place (85 degrees), free from drafts, one hour and 40 minutes or until double in bulk. Divide dough between two greased 9"x5" loaf pans. Sprinkle loaves with turbinado sugar. Bake at 375 degrees for 25 minutes, or until loaves sound hollow when tapped. Remove from pans. Cool on a wire rack. Makes 2 loaves.

Whole-Wheat
Popovers

# Whole-Wheat Popovers

*Also called Laplanders and puff pops, popovers are considered an Americanized version of England's Yorkshire pudding.*

½ c. all-purpose flour
½ c. whole-wheat flour
¼ t. salt
1 c. reduced-fat milk

2 eggs
2 egg whites
1 T. oil

Combine flours and salt in a medium bowl. Whisk together milk, eggs, egg whites and oil in a separate bowl. Whisk milk mixture into flour mixture, whisking until smooth. Place a popover pan or six 8-ounce custard cups heavily coated with non-stick vegetable spray on a baking sheet. Place in a 425-degree oven 3 minutes or until hot. Remove baking sheet from oven and fill cups half full with batter. Bake at 425 degrees for 30 minutes. Turn oven off; remove pan from oven. Cut a small slit in top of each popover; return to oven. Let popovers stand in closed oven 3 minutes. Serve immediately. Makes 6.

# Herbed Fan Dinner Rolls

*When baked, the layers of the roll spread out to mimic a fan.*

¼ c. butter or margarine, melted
½ t. dried Italian seasoning

11-oz. pkg. refrigerated bread dough

Combine butter and Italian seasoning in a small bowl, stirring well. Roll dough into a 13-inch square. Cut into 4 equal strips. Stack strips on top of each other. Cut strips crosswise into 6 equal stacks. Place each stack, cut-side up, in a greased muffin cup; brush with butter mixture. Cover and let rise in a warm place (85 degrees), free from drafts, 25 minutes or until double in bulk. Bake at 375 degrees for 22 to 25 minutes, until golden. Brush with butter mixture again, if desired. Makes 6.

## make-ahead magic

Place dough pieces in muffin cups; brush with butter mixture. Cover and freeze. Thaw, covered, in a warm place 2 hours, or until double in bulk. Bake as directed.

# Jack-o'-Lantern Bread

*Follow package directions for thawing bread dough. If making ahead, wrap cooled bread airtight and keep at room temperature up to one day or freeze to store longer. Reheat (thaw, if frozen), loosely wrapped in aluminum foil, in a 350-degree oven 10 to 15 minutes, until warm.*

2 1-lb. loaves frozen bread dough, thawed

1 T. beaten egg
1½ t. milk

Place the loaves in a bowl. Cover bowl with plastic wrap and let rise until double in bulk, 45 minutes to one hour. Punch dough down, knead loaves together in bowl and shape into a ball. Transfer ball to a greased 15"x12" baking sheet. With greased hands or a lightly floured rolling pin, flatten ball into a 13-inch by 11-inch oval. Cut out eyes and mouth; openings should be at least 1½ to 2 inches wide. (To make small loaves, divide dough into 4 equal pieces and roll into 6-inch by 4-inch ovals; eye and mouth openings should be at least one to 1½ inches wide.) Lift out cut-out dough and bake on another baking sheet or use for decoration. Cover the shaped dough lightly with plastic wrap and let rise until puffy, about 20 minutes. Mix egg with milk in a small bowl; brush over dough. Bake at 350 degrees for 30 to 35 minutes, until golden. Cool on a wire rack. Serve warm or cooled. Serves 10 to 12.

Vickie
Gooseberry Patch

# Best-Ever Soft Pretzels

1½ c. water
1 env. active dry yeast
1 T. sugar
2 t. salt

4 c. all-purpose flour
1 egg yolk
1 T. water
¼ c. coarse salt

Heat 1½ cups water until very warm, about 110 to 115 degrees. Combine with yeast in a large bowl. Stir in sugar and salt until dissolved. Add flour; mix well. Turn dough out onto a floured surface; knead 5 minutes. Divide dough into 16 equal pieces. Roll into thin strips; shape into pretzels. Place on a well-greased baking sheet. Beat egg yolk with one tablespoon water in a small bowl; brush over pretzels. Sprinkle with salt; bake at 425 degrees for 15 to 20 minutes, until golden. Makes 16.

Vickie
Gooseberry Patch

# Harvest Pumpkin Bread

*Dress up this bread with raisins or walnuts, if you like.*

2 c. all-purpose flour, divided
1 c. brown sugar, packed
1 t. cinnamon
¼ t. nutmeg
⅛ t. ground cloves
1 T. baking powder
¼ t. baking soda

¼ t. salt
1 c. canned pumpkin
½ c. milk
⅓ c. butter or margarine,
    softened
2 eggs

Combine one cup flour, brown sugar, cinnamon, nutmeg, cloves, baking powder, baking soda and salt in a mixing bowl. Add pumpkin, milk, butter and eggs and beat with an electric mixer at low speed until blended; increase speed to high and beat 2 minutes. Gradually add remaining flour and beat until well mixed. Pour batter into a greased 9"x5" loaf pan and bake for one hour to 65 minutes. Makes one loaf.

# White Christmas Coconut Sheet Cake

18¼-oz. pkg. white cake mix
¾ c. cream of coconut
¼ c. butter, melted
3 eggs
½ c. water
¾ c. lemon curd
4 1-oz. sqs. white baking
   chocolate, chopped
½ c. sour cream
1 c. whipping cream
¼ c. powdered sugar
6-oz. pkg. frozen grated
   coconut, thawed
Optional: maraschino cherries
   with stems, lemon zest

## make-ahead magic

This cake can be made ahead and stored in the refrigerator for up to 3 days.

Combine cake mix, cream of coconut, butter, eggs and water in a large bowl; beat with an electric mixer at low speed for one minute. Increase speed to medium and beat 1½ minutes. Spread batter into a greased and floured 13"x9" baking pan. Bake at 350 degrees for 35 minutes, or until a toothpick inserted in center comes out clean. Remove pan to a wire rack; spread lemon curd over hot cake. Cool completely in pan on wire rack. (Cake will sink slightly in center.) Place white chocolate in a small microwave-safe bowl; microwave, uncovered, on high one minute, or until melted, stirring after 30 seconds. Stir in sour cream. Cover and chill 30 minutes. Beat whipping cream and powdered sugar in a large bowl at medium speed until stiff peaks form. Add white chocolate mixture and beat at low speed just until combined. Spread whipped cream topping over cake; sprinkle with coconut. Cover and chill 8 hours. Garnish with maraschino cherries and lemon zest, if desired. Store, covered, in refrigerator. Serves 15.

Jo Ann
Gooseberry Patch

# Jumbo Chocolate Cupcakes

1 c. butter, softened
1 c. light brown sugar, packed
½ c. sugar
4 eggs
3 1-oz. sqs. unsweetened
　baking chocolate, melted
1 t. vanilla extract

2 c. all-purpose flour
1 t. baking soda
½ t. salt
1 c. buttermilk
12 Christmas-themed cupcake
　toppers

Beat butter in a large bowl with an electric mixer at medium speed until creamy. Gradually add sugars, beating well. Add eggs, one at a time, beating after each addition. Add melted chocolate and vanilla, beating well. Combine flour, baking soda and salt in a separate bowl; add to batter alternately with buttermilk, beginning and ending with flour mixture. Beat at low speed after each addition until blended. Spoon batter into paper-lined jumbo muffin cups, filling three-quarters full. Bake at 350 degrees for 30 minutes, or until a toothpick inserted in center comes out clean. Cool in pans on wire racks 5 minutes. Remove from pans and cool completely on wire racks 45 minutes. Spread with Thick Chocolate Frosting. Insert one topper into top of each cupcake. Makes one dozen.

## Thick Chocolate Frosting:

½ c. butter, softened
16-oz. pkg. powdered sugar
1 c. semi-sweet chocolate
　chips, melted

½ c. whipping cream
2 t. vanilla extract
⅛ t. salt

Beat butter in a large bowl with an electric mixer at medium speed until creamy; gradually add powdered sugar alternately with melted chocolate and whipping cream. Beat at low speed after each addition until blended. Stir in vanilla and salt. Makes 3½ cups.

# Patriotic Cupcakes

## make-ahead magic

To make ahead, bake and cool cupcakes as directed. Do not frost and decorate. Double-wrap cupcakes in plastic wrap and heavy-duty aluminum foil or place in airtight containers; freeze up to one month.

2 c. sugar
1 c. butter, softened
2 eggs
2 t. lemon juice
1 t. vanilla extract

2½ c. cake flour
½ t. baking soda
1 c. buttermilk
24 mini American flags

Beat sugar and butter in a large bowl with an electric mixer at medium speed until creamy. Add eggs, one at a time, beating until yellow disappears after each addition. Beat in lemon juice and vanilla. Combine flour and baking soda in a small bowl; add to sugar mixture alternately with buttermilk, beginning and ending with flour mixture. Beat at medium speed just until blended after each addition. Spoon batter into paper-lined muffin cups, filling two-thirds full. Bake at 350 degrees for 18 to 22 minutes, until a toothpick inserted in center comes out clean. Cool in pans on a wire rack 10 minutes. Remove cupcakes from pans to wire rack; cool 45 minutes, or until completely cool. Spoon 5-Cup Cream Cheese Frosting into a plastic zipping bag (do not seal). Snip one bottom corner of bag to make a hole (about one inch in diameter). Pipe frosting in little loops onto tops of cupcakes as desired. Insert one flag into top of each cupcake. Makes 2 dozen.

## 5-Cup Cream Cheese Frosting:

2 8-oz. pkgs. cream cheese, softened
½ c. butter, softened

2 16-oz. pkgs. powdered sugar
2 t. vanilla extract

Beat cream cheese and butter with an electric mixer at medium speed until creamy. Gradually add powdered sugar, beating until fluffy. Stir in vanilla. Makes about 5 cups.

# Perfect Pecan Pie

3 eggs
½ c. sugar
¼ t. salt
3 T. butter, melted
1 c. dark corn syrup

1 t. vanilla extract
2 c. pecan halves
9-inch frozen pie crust
Optional: vanilla ice cream

Whisk together eggs, sugar, salt, butter, corn syrup and vanilla in a bowl until thoroughly blended. Stir in pecans. Fit pie crust into a 9" pie plate according to package directions. Fold edges under and crimp. Pour filling into pie crust. Bake on lower rack at 350 degrees for 40 minutes, or until pie is set, covering edges with aluminum foil after 15 minutes. Cool completely on a wire rack. Serve with vanilla ice cream, if desired. Serves 6.

# Chocolate Chess Pie

½ c. margarine
1½ 1-oz. sqs. unsweetened
  baking chocolate, chopped
1 c. brown sugar, packed
½ c. sugar
2 eggs, beaten

1 t. all-purpose flour
1 T. milk
1 t. vanilla extract
9-inch frozen pie crust
Optional: whipped cream

*"My favorite winter recipe...Mom always made it at Christmas."*

*–Heidi Jo*

Melt margarine and chocolate in a small saucepan over low heat; set aside. Combine sugars, eggs, flour, milk and vanilla in a medium bowl. Gradually add chocolate mixture, beating constantly. Pour into pie crust; bake at 325 degrees for 40 to 45 minutes. Cool before serving. Top with whipped cream, if desired. Serves 6 to 8.

Heidi Jo McManaman
Grand Rapids, MI

Candy Corn-Popcorn Balls

# Candy Corn-Popcorn Balls

*Full of popcorn and candy corn, this treat will be a hit! You'll need to work quickly to shape the balls, so gather everyone to help.*

6 qts. popped popcorn
2 c. sugar
1 c. corn syrup
1 T. butter

½ t. cream of tartar
½ t. baking soda
1 to 1½ c. candy corn

## toss-ins for a twist

You can also substitute gummy worms or gummy bears for the candy corn in this holiday favorite.

Place popcorn in a large bowl. Heat sugar, corn syrup, butter and cream of tartar in a heavy saucepan to 270 degrees on a candy thermometer (hard-ball stage); remove from heat. Carefully stir in baking soda. Pour sugar mixture over popped popcorn; toss to coat. When just cool enough to handle, mix in candy corn and shape into 3-inch balls using buttered hands. Set aside to cool completely. Wrap individually in plastic wrap or cellophane; store in an airtight container. Makes 16.

Megan Tkacik
New Castle, PA

# Snowflake Press Cookies

*Dust baked cookies with sanding sugar for sparkle!*

½ c. butter, softened
½ c. shortening
3-oz. pkg. cream cheese, softened
1 c. sugar
1 egg yolk

1 t. orange zest
1 t. vanilla extract
2½ c. all-purpose flour
½ t. salt
¼ t. cinnamon

Blend butter, shortening and cream cheese in a large bowl; add sugar, egg yolk, orange zest and vanilla. Mix well; set aside. Combine flour, salt and cinnamon in a separate bowl; stir into butter mixture. Chill 30 minutes; place dough in a cookie press. Form snowflakes one inch apart on ungreased baking sheets. Bake at 350 degrees for 12 to 15 minutes. Makes 4 dozen.

Liz Hall
Worthington, IN

# Chocolate Granola Brittle

*The beauty of this recipe is that you can make a decadent brittle in the microwave in half the time it takes to make the traditional candy. If you want to make more than one pound, don't double the recipe…it won't give you the same result. Just make it twice.*

1 c. sugar
½ c. light corn syrup
⅛ t. salt
1 c. pecans, coarsely chopped
1 T. butter
1 t. vanilla extract

1 t. baking soda
¾ c. chocolate granola
3 1-oz. sqs. semi-sweet baking chocolate
1½ T. shortening

Combine sugar, corn syrup and salt in a 2-quart glass bowl. Microwave, uncovered, on high 5 minutes. Stir in pecans. Microwave 1½ minutes. Stir in butter and vanilla. Microwave one minute and 45 seconds or until candy is the color of peanut butter. Stir in baking soda (mixture will bubble). Quickly pour candy onto a lightly greased rimless baking sheet. (Pour as thinly as possible without spreading candy.) Cover brittle quickly with parchment paper and use a rolling pin to thin out candy; peel off parchment. Sprinkle granola over brittle. Cool brittle completely; break into pieces. Place chocolate squares and shortening in a small microwave-safe bowl. Microwave, uncovered, on high 1½ to 2 minutes, stirring after one minute. Dip each piece of brittle halfway into chocolate mixture. Place dipped brittle on parchment paper to harden. Store in an airtight container. Makes about one pound.

## party favors

Package treats, such as candied nuts, fudge, almond brittle, cookies or brownies, in airtight containers and then slip them into gift bags tied with ribbon or raffia. Set them in a basket by your door so there will always be a treat waiting for guests to take home.

# METRIC EQUIVALENTS

The recipes that appear in this cookbook use the standard U.S. method for measuring liquid and dry or solid ingredients (teaspoons, tablespoons, and cups). The information in the following charts is provided to help cooks outside the United States successfully use these recipes. All equivalents are approximate.

## METRIC EQUIVALENTS FOR DIFFERENT TYPES OF INGREDIENTS

A standard cup measure of a dry or solid ingredient will vary in weight depending on the type of ingredient. A standard cup of liquid is the same volume for any type of liquid. Use the following chart when converting standard cup measures to grams (weight) or milliliters (volume).

| Standard Cup | Fine Powder (ex. flour) | Grain (ex. rice) | Granular (ex. sugar) | Liquid Solids (ex. butter) | Liquid (ex. milk) |
|---|---|---|---|---|---|
| 1 | 140 g | 150 g | 190 g | 200 g | 240 ml |
| ¾ | 105 g | 113 g | 143 g | 150 g | 180 ml |
| ⅔ | 93 g | 100 g | 125 g | 133 g | 160 ml |
| ½ | 70 g | 75 g | 95 g | 100 g | 120 ml |
| ⅓ | 47 g | 50 g | 63 g | 67 g | 80 ml |
| ¼ | 35 g | 38 g | 48 g | 50 g | 60 ml |
| ⅛ | 18 g | 19 g | 24 g | 25 g | 30 ml |

## USEFUL EQUIVALENTS FOR LIQUID INGREDIENTS BY VOLUME

| | | | | |
|---|---|---|---|---|
| ¼ tsp | = | | | 1 ml |
| ½ tsp | = | | | 2 ml |
| 1 tsp | = | | | 5 ml |
| 3 tsp | = 1 Tbsp | | = ½ fl oz | = 15 ml |
| | 2 Tbsp | = ⅛ c | = 1 fl oz | = 30 ml |
| | 4 Tbsp | = ¼ c | = 2 fl oz | = 60 ml |
| | 5⅓ Tbsp | = ⅓ c | = 3 fl oz | = 80 ml |
| | 8 Tbsp | = ½ c | = 4 fl oz | = 120 ml |
| | 10⅔ Tbsp | = ⅔ c | = 5 fl oz | = 160 ml |
| | 12 Tbsp | = ¾ c | = 6 fl oz | = 180 ml |
| | 16 Tbsp | = 1 c | = 8 fl oz | = 240 ml |
| | 1 pt | = 2 c | = 16 fl oz | = 480 ml |
| | 1 qt | = 4 c | = 32 fl oz | = 960 ml |
| | | | 33 fl oz | = 1000 ml = 1 liter |

## USEFUL EQUIVALENTS FOR DRY INGREDIENTS BY WEIGHT

(To convert ounces to grams, multiply the number of ounces by 30.)

| | | | | |
|---|---|---|---|---|
| 1 oz | = | 1/16 lb | = | 30 g |
| 4 oz | = | ¼ lb | = | 120 g |
| 8 oz | = | ½ lb | = | 240 g |
| 12 oz | = | ¾ lb | = | 360 g |
| 16 oz | = | 1 lb | = | 480 g |

## USEFUL EQUIVALENTS FOR LENGTH

(To convert inches to centimeters, multiply the number of inches by 2.5.)

| | | | | |
|---|---|---|---|---|
| 1 in | | | = | 2.5 cm |
| 6 in | = ½ ft | | = | 15 cm |
| 12 in | = 1 ft | | = | 30 cm |
| 36 in | = 3 ft | = 1 yd | = | 90 cm |
| 40 in | | | = 100 cm | = 1 meter |

## USEFUL EQUIVALENTS FOR COOKING/OVEN TEMPERATURES

| | Fahrenheit | Celsius | Gas Mark |
|---|---|---|---|
| Freeze Water | 32° F | 0° C | |
| Room Temperature | 68° F | 20° C | |
| Boil Water | 212° F | 100° C | |
| Bake | 325° F | 160° C | 3 |
| | 350° F | 180° C | 4 |
| | 375° F | 190° C | 5 |
| | 400° F | 200° C | 6 |
| | 425° F | 220° C | 7 |
| | 450° F | 230° C | 8 |
| Broil | | | Grill |

# index

## soups & stews

## sandwiches

## sides

# Everyday Comfort Food

ISBN-13: 978-0-8487-4223-2
ISBN-10: 0-8487-4223-0

Library of Congress Control Number: 2013941124
Printed in the United States of America
First Printing 2013

**Oxmoor House**
Editorial Director: Leah McLaughlin
Creative Director: Felicity Keane
Brand Manager: Vanessa Tiongson
Senior Editor: Rebecca Brennan

### *Gooseberry Patch Everyday Comfort Food*

Editor: Susan Ray
Art Director: Claire Cormany
Project Editor: Emily Chappell Connolly
Assistant Designer: Allison Sperando Potter
Director, Test Kitchen: Elizabeth Tyler Austin
Recipe Developers and Testers: Wendy Ball, R.D.; Victoria E. Cox; Tamara Goldis; Stefanie Maloney; Callie Nash; Karen Rankin; Leah Van Deren
Recipe Editor: Alyson Moreland Haynes
Food Stylists: Margaret Monroe Dickey, Catherine Crowell Steele
Photography Director: Jim Bathie
Senior Photographer: Hélène Dujardin
Senior Photo Stylist: Kay E. Clarke
Photo Stylist: Mindi Shapiro Levine
Assistant Photo Stylist: Mary Louise Menendez
Production Manager: Theresa Beste-Farley
Associate Production Manager: Kimberly Marshall

**Contributors**
Project Editor: Melissa Brown
Recipe Developers and Testers: Erica Hopper, Tonya Johnson, Kyra Moncrief
Copy Editors: Jasmine Hodges, Rhonda Lee Lother
Interns: Megan Branagh, Frances Gunnells, Susan Kemp, Sara Lyon, Staley McIlwain, Jeffrey Preis, Maria Sanders, Julia Sayers
Food Stylist: Ana Price Kelley, Kathleen Royal Phillips
Photographer: Becky Stayner
Photo Stylist: Mary Clayton Carl, Melanie Clarke

**Time Home Entertainment Inc.**
Publisher: Jim Childs
VP, Brand & Digital Strategy: Steven Sandonato
Executive Director, Marketing Services: Carol Pittard
Executive Director, Retail & Special Sales: Tom Mifsud
Director, Bookazine Development & Marketing: Laura Adam
Executive Publishing Director: Joy Butts
Associate Publishing Director: Megan Pearlman
Finance Director: Glenn Buonocore
Associate General Counsel: Helen Wan

To order additional publications,
call 1-800-765-6400 or 1-800-491-0551.

For more books to enrich your life, visit **oxmoorhouse.com**

To search, savor, and share thousands of recipes,
visit **myrecipes.com**

Front Cover (from left to right, top to bottom):
Bread Pudding (page 192), Fix & Forget Stuffed Peppers (page 98), Easy Cheesy Manicotti (page 148)

Page 1: Chicken, Lime & Tortilla Soup (page 113)

Back Cover (from left to right, top to bottom): Overnight Buttermilk-Raisin Pancakes (page 38), Fajitas (page 93), Chocolate Chess Pie (page 245)

## Our Story

Back in 1984, we were next-door neighbors raising our families in the little town of Delaware, Ohio. Two moms with small children, we were looking for a way to do what we loved and stay home with the kids too. We had always shared a love of home cooking and making memories with family & friends and so, after many a conversation over the backyard fence, **Gooseberry Patch** was born.

We put together our first catalog at our kitchen tables, enlisting the help of our loved ones wherever we could. From that very first mailing, we found an immediate connection with many of our customers, and it wasn't long before we began receiving letters, photos and recipes from these new friends. In 1992, we put together our very first cookbook, compiled from hundreds of these recipes, and the rest, as they say, is history.

Hard to believe it's been over 25 years since those kitchen-table days! From that original little **Gooseberry Patch** family, we've grown to include an amazing group of creative folks who love cooking, decorating and creating as much as we do. Today, we're best known for our homestyle, family-friendly cookbooks, now recognized as national bestsellers.

One thing's for sure, we couldn't have done it without our friends all across the country. Each year, we're honored to turn thousands of your recipes into our collectible cookbooks. Our hope is that each book captures the stories and heart of all of you who have shared with us. Whether you've been with us since the beginning or are just discovering us, welcome to the **Gooseberry Patch** family!

### We couldn't make our best-selling cookbooks without YOU!

Each of our books is filled with recipes from cooks just like you, gathered from kitchens all across the country.

Share your tried & true recipes with us on our website and you could be selected for an upcoming cookbook. If your recipe is included, you'll receive a FREE copy of the cookbook when it's published!

## www.gooseberrypatch.com

### We'd love to add YOU to our Circle of Friends!

Get free recipes, crafts, giveaways and so much more when you join our email club...join us online at all the spots below for even more goodies!